Reading
EXPLORER
INTRO

Becky Tarver Chase • Kristin L. Johannsen

NATIONAL
GEOGRAPHIC
LEARNING

HEINLE
CENGAGE Learning®

Australia • Brazil • Japan • Korea • Mexico • Singapore • Spain • United Kingdom • United States

Reading Explorer Intro
Becky Tarver Chase and Kristin L. Johannsen

VP and Director of Operations: Vincent Grosso

Publisher: Andrew Robinson

Executive Editor: Sean Bermingham

Senior Development Editor: Derek Mackrell

Assistant Editor: Sarah Tan

Senior Technology Development Manager: Debie Mirtle

Technology Project Manager: Shi-May Wei

Director of Global Marketing: Ian Martin

Director of US Marketing: Jim McDonough

Content Project Manager: Tan Jin Hock

Print Buyer: Susan Spencer

National Geographic Coordinator: Leila Hishmeh

Cover/Text Designer: Page 2, LLC

Compositor: Page 2, LLC

Cover Images: (Top) Michael Melford/National Geographic Image Collection, (bottom) Steve Winter/National Geographic Image Collection

Credits appear on page 160, which constitutes a continuation of the copyright page.

Acknowledgments

The Author and Publishers would like to thank the following teaching professionals for their valuable feedback during the development of this series.

Jamie Ahn, English Coach, Seoul; **Heidi Bundschoks**, ITESM, Sinaloa México; José Olavo de Amorim, Colégio Bandeirantes, São Paulo; **Marina Gonzalez**, Instituto Universitario de Lenguas Modernas Pte., Buenos Aires; **Tsung-Yuan Hsiao**, National Taiwan Ocean University, Keelung; **Michael Johnson**, Muroran Institute of Technology; **Thays Ladosky**, Colégio Damas, Recife; **Ahmed Mohamed Motala**, University of Sharjah; **Mae-Ran Park**, Pukyong National University, Busan; **David Persey**, British Council, Bangkok; **David Schneer**, ACS International, Singapore; **Atsuko Takase**, Kinki University, Osaka; **Deborah E. Wilson**, American University of Sharjah

Additional thanks to Diana Jaksic, Jim McClelland, and Jim Burch at National Geographic Society.

This series is dedicated to the memory of Joe Dougherty, who was a constant inspiration throughout its development.

Student Book ISBN-13: 978-1-111-05576-9

Student Book ISBN-10: 1-111-05576-9

Student Book + Student CD-ROM ISBN-13: 978-1-111-06434-1

Student Book + Student CD-ROM ISBN-10: 1-111-06434-2

Student Book (US edition) ISBN-13: 978-1-111-05708-4

Student Book (US edition) ISBN-10: 1-111-05708-7

National Geographic Learning
20 Channel Center Street
Boston, MA 02210
USA

Cengage Learning is a leading provider of customized learning solutions with office locations around the globe, including Singapore, the United Kingdom, Australia, Mexico, Brazil, and Japan.

Cengage Learning products are represented in Canada by Nelson Education, Ltd.

Visit National Geographic Learning online at **elt.heinle.com**

Visit our corporate website at **www.cengage.com**

Printed in the United States of America
2 3 4 5 6 7 16 15 14 13 12

Contents

Get ready to Explore Your World!

Yellowstone is America's oldest national park. It is also the most dangerous. Why? **p. 142**

An explorer's 1985 discovery in the **North Atlantic**, was big news around the world. What did he find? **p. 45**

NORTH AMERICA

The Mexican city of **Oaxaca** is famous for its festivals and its food. Why are they special? **p. 28**

Researchers at the University of **California** are studying dreams. Why do we have dreams—and what do they tell us? **p. 83**

In the **United States**, there are more statues of Sacagawea than any other American woman. Why is she famous today? **p. 65**

SOUTH AMERICA

The **Nazca** lines are one of the wonders of the ancient world. What are they? **p. 40**

In 1533, a great golden treasure was buried in the **Andes** What happened to it? **p. 99**

Ancient writers described an island-city in the **Atlantic Ocean**. But was it real? **p. 15**

The world's richest horse race takes place each year in **Dubai**. What's the prize? **p. 62**

In 2007, a mysterious body was discovered in **Siberia**. Where—and when—did it come from? **p. 123**

Scientists in **South Korea** have developed a new kind of robot called EveR-1. What can it do? **p. 135**

EUROPE

ASIA

AFRICA

Japan's anime films are watched and loved around the world. What makes them so popular? **p. 35**

The Taj Mahal in **Agra**, India has been called the world's most beautiful building. Who built it— and why? **p. 108**

AUSTRALIA

Near Kruger National Park in **South Africa** is a school with a difference. Why is it unusual? **p. 113**

Thousands of people climb **Uluru** every year. Some people think they shouldn't. Why? **p. 74**

ANTARCTICA

Scope and Sequence

Unit	Theme	Lesson	Reading Passage	Vocabulary Building	Video
1	Mysteries	**A:** Aliens and UFOs **B:** Mysterious Places	Have Aliens Visited Us? The Lost Land	Usage: *research* vs. *design* Word Link: *–al*	**Loch Ness Mystery**
2	Favorite Foods	**A:** Slices of History **B:** Sugar and Spice	Where Is Pizza From? The Hottest Chili	Usage: *learn* vs. *teach* Word Partnership: *break*	**A Taste of Mexico**
3	That's Entertainment!	**A:** Animal Actors **B:** Making Movies	My Grizzly Summer Job The Master of Anime	Usage: *human* Usage: *the media*	**History of Film**
Review 1	Mystery Lines	**World Heritage Spotlight:** Nasca Lines, Peru		Dictionary Skills Word Link: *–ly*	
4	True Tales	**A:** Titanic **B:** Danger!	"I've Found the Titanic" "I Was Struck by Lightning!"	Usage: *agree* Word Partnership: *rule*	**Lightning**
5	Outdoor Activities	**A:** Baseball **B:** Outdoor Adventure	Baseball Goes Global Hiking in Korea	Word Link: *–er* Usage: *enjoy*	**Dubai World Cup**
6	History and Legends	**A:** Real-Life Legends **B:** Stories and Myths	Who Was Sacagawea? A Tale of the Dreamtime	Usage: *town* vs. *village* vs. *city* Word Partnership: *meeting*	**Native Americans**
Review 2	Rock of Legends	**World Heritage Spotlight:** Uluru-Kata Tjuta National Park (Ayers Rock), Australia		Dictionary Skills Word Link: *–er / –or*	

Introduction

Welcome to Reading Explorer!

In this book, you'll travel the world, explore different cultures, and discover interesting topics. You'll also become a better reader!

Reading will be easier—and you'll understand more—if you ask yourself these questions:

What do I already know?
- Before you read, look at the photos, captions, charts, and maps. Ask yourself: *What do I already know about this topic?*
- Think about the language you know—or may need to know— to understand the topic.

What do I want to learn?
- Look at the title and headings. Ask yourself: *What is this passage about? What will I learn?*
- As you read, check your predictions.

What have I learned?
- As you read, take notes. Use them to help you answer questions about the passage.
- Write down words you learn in a vocabulary notebook.

How can I learn more?
- Practice your reading skills and vocabulary in the Review Units.
- Explore the topics by watching the videos in class, or at home using the CD-ROM.

Now you're ready to explore your world!

title   photo

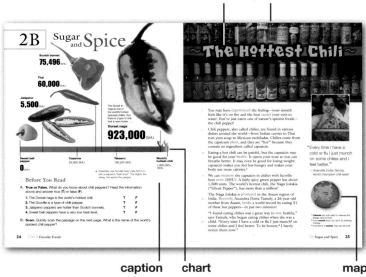

caption   chart   map

UNIT 1
Mysteries

Discuss these questions with a partner.

1. Do you know of any famous mysteries?

2. Has anything strange or mysterious ever happened to you?

3. Do you think that there are things that science cannot explain?

▲ The Northern Lights, also known as the Aurora Borealis, create mysterious patterns in the skies over Alaska, U.S.A.

1A Aliens and UFOs

Before You Read

▲ Science-fiction (sci-fi) movies like *Close Encounters of the Third Kind* make UFOs seem real. But have aliens really been to our world?

A. Discussion. Look at the photos and captions on this and the next page. Then answer the questions below.

1. Do you **believe** in UFOs?[1] (Do **aliens** from space really visit Earth?)
2. Have you ever seen a UFO, or have you heard about UFO **sightings** where you live?
3. If you saw strange lights or **disks** ("flying saucers") in the sky, what would you think?
4. Do you think governments keep **secrets** about UFO visits?

[1] **UFO** = Unidentified Flying Object

B. Skim for Gist. Quickly skim the passage on the next page. What is the passage mainly about? Circle **a**, **b**, or **c**. Then read the passage to check your answer.

a. a famous place for UFO sightings
b. UFO sightings around the world
c. famous movies about UFOs

HAVE ALIENS VISITED US?

▲ An alien model at a UFO museum in Roswell, New Mexico

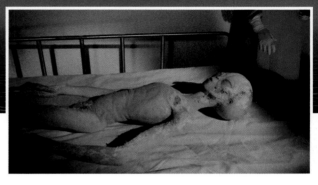

THE STORIES

Judy Varns works for the Mutual UFO Network. The purpose of this group is to research UFO sightings. According to[1] Varns, a place in Nevada called Area 51 may be the best place on Earth to see a UFO. She took some photos in the area. In the images she saw something that she thinks is a UFO. "We saw this little disk-shaped thing in our photos. It's kind of exciting," she says.

Pat Travis lives near Area 51. One night she saw a strange light in the sky. The light's movement was very unusual. "It [went] sideways. It [went] up, down," she says. "It [made] these strange kinds of moves." Travis thinks it was a UFO from space.

▲ Is Area 51 really the best place on Earth to see a UFO?

WHAT IS AREA 51?

The US Air Force[2] uses Area 51 for testing new technology. Area 51 is not really the airport's name—its real name is a secret. James McGaha, a pilot who flew airplanes at Area 51, says, "There is absolutely[3] no UFO activity" at Area 51 . . . "No flying saucers, no live aliens, no dead aliens."

So what did Varns and Travis see?

Bill Fox helped to design new airplanes at Area 51. He thinks he knows the answer. "We did build some strange-looking airplanes," he says. "I could see why some people would think they were UFOs."

Are UFOs real? You'll have to decide for yourself. But if you visit southern Nevada, keep your eyes on the skies!

Area 51,
Nevada,
U.S.A.

---

[1] If something is true **according to** someone, it is said or stated by that person.
[2] An **air force** is part of a country's military that fights in the air.
[3] **Absolutely** means totally or completely.

☐ Reading Comprehension

A. Multiple Choice. Choose the best answer for each question.

Detail **1.** Which sentence about Judy Varns is true?
   a. She helped Bill Fox design new airplanes.
   b. She works at an airport in Nevada.
   c. She doesn't believe UFOs are real.
   d. She works for a group that studies UFO sightings.

Main Idea **2.** What is the main idea of the second paragraph (from line 10)?
   a. Pat Travis lives near Area 51.
   b. Pat Travis has seen many unusual things.
   c. Pat Travis thinks she saw a UFO.
   d. Pat Travis thinks UFOs are from space.

Vocabulary **3.** In line 13, the word *kinds* is closest in meaning to _____.
   a. lines
   b. groups
   c. friends
   d. types

Detail **4.** What was James McGaha's job at Area 51?
   a. He made airplanes.
   b. He looked for aliens.
   c. He flew airplanes.
   d. He took secret photos.

Paraphrase **5.** What does *I could see why some people would think they were UFOs* (line 24) mean?
   a. I understand why some people think they saw UFOs.
   b. I agree with people who believe in UFOs.
   c. I could see UFOs near Area 51 with my own eyes.
   d. I don't know whether UFOs are real or not.

B. Matching. Match each statement (**a–d**) with the person who probably said it.

1. _____ Judy Varns
2. _____ Bill Fox
3. _____ James McGaha
4. _____ Pat Travis

   a. "The airplanes we made might have looked like UFOs to some people."
   b. "Look at these pictures! Do you think that's a UFO?"
   c. "I believe in UFOs. I saw one with my own eyes."
   d. "I used to fly airplanes at Area 51. There are no UFOs there."

Vocabulary Practice

A. Matching. Read the information below. Then match each word in red with its definition.

Crop circles have been seen in the U.K., Australia, Russia, and about 50 other countries. But how—and for what purpose—are they made? A family in a quiet farmland area wakes up one morning to find something very unusual: someone has cut strange shapes into their crop fields! These huge designs are called crop circles. There are circles, stars, even images of animals. But where do these crop circles come from?

Some people think that UFOs make crop circles when they land in fields. Others say they are made by aliens from space, but no one knows the purpose.

Another—more realistic—idea is that some people decide to build crop circles as a hobby, or as a kind of art. The technology to make crop circles is very simple—just a rope and a piece of wood. Some teachers and students have built crop circles for fun.

Crop circles are real—there are photographs and reports of about 12,000 of them. But more research is needed before we really know how and why these shapes are made.

1. to make something _____
2. a pattern, shape, or plan _____
3. a picture of a person or thing _____
4. to choose to do something _____
5. a place, part, or region _____
6. the reason for doing something _____
7. true or actual _____
8. trying to discover facts about something _____
9. outside the Earth; where stars and planets are _____
10. using science and machines to do things _____

B. Words in Context. Complete each sentence with the best answer.

1. Research is an important part of a(n) _____'s job.
   a. scientist   b. artist
2. An example of technology is a _____.
   a. computer   b. song
3. The purpose of *Reading Explorer* is to _____.
   a. have 160 pages   b. help you read better
4. You can _____ an image of a bird.
   a. see   b. hear

▲ Crop circles are popular with tourists. "We get tens of thousands of people coming to the U.K. each year just to look at them," says Karen Alexander, co-author of *Crop Circles: Signs, Wonders, and Mysteries.*

Usage

Both **research** and **design** can be used as a noun and a verb: *Professor Baker is **researching** UFOs. His **research** will take five years.*
*What do you think of my new **design**? I **designed** it myself.*

1B Mysterious Places

◀ For thousands of years people have tried to place Atlantis on a map. But no one really knows if the island was real.

Before You Read

A. Matching. Read the information below and match each word in **blue** with its definition.

Long ago, the Greek writer Plato (pictured above) wrote about Atlantis — an **island** that **disappeared** into the sea. No one has found Atlantis, but there are many stories about it. In the stories, the Atlantean people were very **wealthy**, but also very **greedy** — they wanted too much, so they lost everything.

1. _____ wanting a lot of money, food, etc.[1]
2. _____ rich; having a lot of money
3. _____ a piece of land with water all around it
4. _____ to go out of sight

[1] **etc.** (et cetera) = and other things; and so on

B. Scan. Quickly scan the passage on the next page. Look for answers to these questions:

1. Whose names can you find in the passage?
2. Which places are mentioned in the passage?

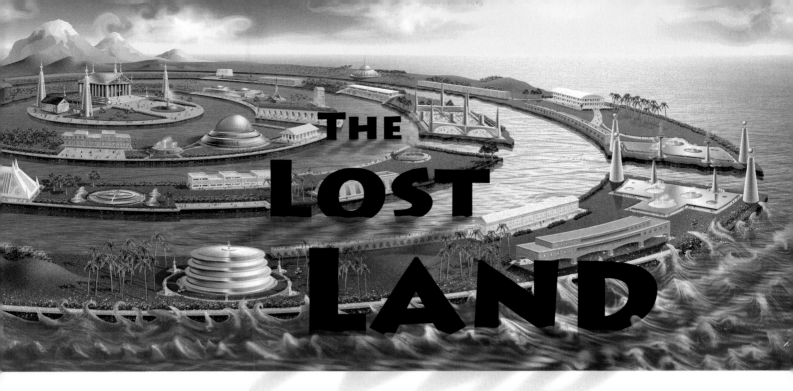

THE LOST LAND

1   Most people have heard the story of the lost island of Atlantis. But is any part of the story true?

  The Greek writer Plato wrote that Atlantis was an island in the Atlantic Ocean. The island's wealthy people designed many great
5   buildings and canals.[1] At the center of the island they built a beautiful golden temple.[2] But the Atlanteans became greedy— they had everything, but they still wanted more. The gods became angry, and the island was hit by earthquakes[3] and great waves. Finally, the whole of Atlantis sank into the sea.

10   Throughout history, explorers have reported finding Atlantis. In 2004, the explorer Robert Sarmast reported finding the island's remains[4] on an undersea mountain near Cyprus. However, Sarmast and other scientists later found out these findings were natural, not man-made.

15   Many people think Atlantis is simply a story. The purpose of the story was to teach people about the evils[5] of greed. Richard Ellis published a book on Atlantis in 1999. He says "there is not a piece of solid evidence"[6] for a real Atlantis.

20   So was the island real or not? Only one thing is certain: the mystery of Atlantis will be with us for a long time.

> "There were a great number of elephants in the island, for there was [enough] food for all sorts of animals."
> —*Plato (427–347 B.C.)*

---

[1] A **canal** is a long, man-made waterway, often used for boats.
[2] A **temple** is a building where people practice a religion (Buddhism, Judaism, etc.).
[3] An **earthquake** is a shaking of the ground caused by movement of the Earth's crust.
[4] The **remains** of something are the parts that are left after most have been taken away, or destroyed.
[5] **Evil** means all the very bad things that happen in the world.
[6] **Evidence** is anything that makes you believe that something is true or has really happened.

☐ Reading Comprehension

A. Multiple Choice. Choose the best answer for each question.

Gist **1.** Another title for this reading could be _____.
    a. Atlantis Sinks into the Sea
    b. Atlantis: Real Place or Just a Story?
    c. The Greed of the Atlanteans
    d. I Found the Island of Atlantis

Detail **2.** Which sentence about the story of the Atlanteans is NOT true?
    a. They were wealthy.
    b. They built many buildings.
    c. They were greedy.
    d. They became angry.

Vocabulary **3.** We can change the word *great* in line 8 to _____.
    a. very large
    b. very good
    c. very cold
    d. very slow

Main Idea **4.** What is the main idea of the third paragraph (from line 10)?
    a. Atlantis sank near Cyprus.
    b. No one has really found Atlantis.
    c. The real Atlantis was found a long time ago.
    d. Atlantis will be found under water.

Paraphrase **5.** Which of the following is closest in meaning to *"there is not a piece of solid evidence"* for a real Atlantis (lines 18–19)?
    a. There is only one reason to believe the Atlantis story is true.
    b. The story of Atlantis is made up of many small pieces.
    c. There is nothing to make us believe the Atlantis story is true.
    d. The way to find out about Atlantis is by reading books.

B. Sequencing. Number the events in time order from **1–5**. Then retell the Atlantis story to a partner.

_____ Plato writes about Atlantis.

_____ The Atlanteans became wealthy, but greedy.

_____ Richard Ellis writes about Atlantis.

_____ Robert Sarmast reports that he has found Atlantis.

_____ The island of Atlantis disappears.

Vocabulary Practice

A. Completion. Complete the information using the words in the box. One word is extra.

center	certain	final	natural	publish	report

Edinburgh Castle in Scotland is very old—it has been at the **1.** _____ of Scottish history for over 800 years. A few hundred years ago, secret tunnels were discovered under the castle. These tunnels were not **2.** _____; they were probably built by people living there as a way to leave the castle without being seen.

According to one story, a man was sent down into the tunnels to explore. As he went down into the tunnels, he played bagpipes very loudly so people could hear him outside. Suddenly the music stopped . . . and the bagpiper never came out. Today, some people are **3.** _____ that the bagpiper is still down there playing his **4.** _____ song. They **5.** _____ that you can hear bagpipe music on dark nights.

▲ People in Edinburgh have reported hearing a ghost playing the bagpipes, a Scottish musical instrument.

B. Completion. Read the information. Then complete the sentences using the words in red.

Leeds Castle in Kent, England, is called the "Ladies' Castle," because many queens have lived there throughout its long history. Today, the castle is empty—except, perhaps, for the ghost of a big black dog. Some people believe that simply being able to see the dog brings bad luck. But for one woman, the dog brought very good luck.

The woman reported that one day she was sitting by a window in the castle. She looked up and saw a black dog walk through a stone wall near her seat. She got up to look for it—and the whole area where she was sitting fell into the lake[1] below . . . Thanks to the ghost dog, the lucky woman was able to get out of the castle in one piece!

[1] A **lake** is an inland area of (usually fresh) water, larger than a pond or pool.

▲ Can a ghostly black dog really be seen walking within—and through—the walls of England's Leeds Castle?

1. A place that is hundreds of years old has a long _____.

2. According to the woman, a large _____ of the castle fell into the water.

3. No one knows the _____ story about the ghost dog in Leeds Castle.

4. People have _____ seeing many ghosts in English castles over the years.

5. Perhaps the story is false, and the woman was _____ not telling the truth.

Word Link

The suffix **–al** can make a noun into an adjective, e.g.:
nature → natural
music → musical
center → central

Loch Ness Mystery

A. Preview. Look at the photograph and read the information. What do you think the picture shows?

This photograph was first published in London's *Daily Mail* newspaper on April 21, 1934. It is known as "The Surgeon's Photograph," as it was reportedly taken by a London doctor named R. Kenneth Wilson. According to the newspaper report, the photograph was taken in Loch Ness, a famous lake in Scotland.

▲ "The Surgeon's Photograph," 1934.

B. Summarize. Watch the video, *Loch Ness Mystery*. Then complete the summary below using words from the box. Two words are extra.

build	decided	image	reported
center	finally	published	research
certain	history	real	simply

Loch Ness is a lake in Scotland with a long and unusual
1. _____. Many people have **2.** _____ seeing
a monster swimming in its deep waters, but no one could be
3. _____. The newspapers named the monster "Nessie."

In 1934, a black and white **4.** _____ showing Nessie's head
and neck in the water was **5.** _____ in a London
newspaper. Nearly everyone thought it was **6.** _____.
But 60 years later, the truth **7.** _____ came out.

A man named Duke Wetherall had lost his job when he could not get
a photo of Nessie for a newspaper. So he **8.** _____ to
9. _____ his own monster, using a toy submarine.[1]
He **10.** _____ put the "monster" in Loch Ness and took
a picture of it. Wetherall's photo made "Nessie" famous around the
world. But for many years no one knew the true story behind
the picture.

[1] A **submarine** is a type of boat that can move under water.

C. Think About It.

1. Why do you think so many people have reported seeing Nessie?

2. Which things in this unit can scientists explain? Which things can't they explain?

To learn more about mysteries, visit elt.heinle.com/explorer

Favor
Foo

WARM UP

Discuss these questions with a partner.

1. What food is your country most famous for?

2. Are there any foods from other countries that are popular in your own country?

3. What's the hottest (spiciest) food you've ever eaten?

▲ A youn

bread, rice, and pasta

meat, fish, and dairy products

fruit and vegetables

fats, oils, and sweets

▲ Various types of food are grouped together as the slices of a pizza.

Before You Read

A. Discussion. Look at the picture and information above. Then answer the questions below.

1. Why do you think the slices in the picture are of different sizes? Which kinds of foods do you think are healthy? Which foods can be unhealthy?

2. What kinds of fast food are popular in your country? Do you know anything about their history?

B. Predict. Read the title on the next page and the first sentence in each paragraph. Check (✓) the questions that the passage probably answers.

❐ Who made the first pizza? ❐ How many pizzas are eaten every year?

❐ When were tomatoes first used on pizza? ❐ What is the most popular kind of pizza?

Where Is Pizza From?

1 Pizza is certainly one of the world's favorite foods. But where does pizza come from? And who made the first one?

In fact, people have been making pizza for a very long
5 time. People in the Stone Age[1] cooked grains[2] on hot rocks to make dough—the basic ingredient of pizza. Over time, people used the dough as a plate, covering it with various other foods, herbs, and spices. They had developed the world's first pizza.

▲ About five billion pizzas are served around the world every year.

10 In the early 16th century, European explorers brought back the first tomatoes from the Americas. Tomatoes are a standard ingredient in many pizzas today. At first, however, most Europeans thought they were poisonous[3] (in fact, only the leaves and roots[4] are). For about 200
15 years, few people ate them.

Slowly, people learned that tomatoes were safe to eat, as well as tasty. In the early 19th century, cooks in Naples, Italy, started the tradition of putting tomatoes on baking dough. The flat bread soon became popular with poor
20 people all over Naples. In 1830, cooks in Naples took another big step in pizza history—they opened the world's first pizza restaurant.

Today, up to five billion pizzas are served every year around the world. In the U.S. alone, about 350 slices[5]
25 are eaten every second! People may not know it, but every piece is a slice of history.

Naples, Italy

[1] The **Stone Age** is a very early period of human history, where people used tools and weapons made of stone, not metal.
[2] **Grains** are the small, hard seeds of plants such as wheat or corn.
[3] If something is **poisonous**, it will harm or kill you if you swallow it.
[4] The **roots** of a plant are the parts of it that grow under the ground.
[5] A **slice** of something is a small or thin piece that has been cut from a larger piece.

☐ Reading Comprehension

A. Multiple Choice. Choose the best answer for each question.

Main Idea
1. What is the main idea of the passage?
   a. The first pizza was made by Stone Age people.
   b. In the past, some pizza ingredients were poisonous.
   c. Naples, Italy, was an important place in pizza's history.
   d. Pizza has a long history and has changed with time.

Detail
2. For Stone Age people, why was pizza similar to *a plate* (line 7)?
   a. They put other foods on top of pizza dough.
   b. Pizza could be cooked on hot rocks.
   c. They used pizza dough again and again.
   d. Pizza dough gets hard when it is cooked.

Paraphrase
3. In lines 16–17, the phrase *safe to eat, as well as tasty* could be replaced by _____.
   a. only safe when they taste good
   b. safe to eat and they taste good
   c. not safe to eat but they taste good
   d. taste good if they are cooked well

Vocabulary
4. In line 17, *19th century* could be replaced by _____.
   a. 1700s   c. 1900s
   b. 1800s   d. 2000s

Inference
5. Which statement is probably true?
   a. Stone Age people liked tomatoes on pizza.
   b. The first pizza was made almost 200 years ago.
   c. The first pizzas in Naples didn't cost much money.
   d. Tomatoes were popular in Europe in the 16th century.

B. Completion. Complete the chart below. Fill in each blank with one word or number from the reading.

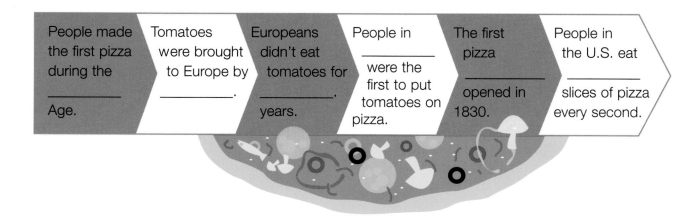

People made the first pizza during the _____ Age. | Tomatoes were brought to Europe by _____. | Europeans didn't eat tomatoes for _____ years. | People in _____ were the first to put tomatoes on pizza. | The first pizza _____ opened in 1830. | People in the U.S. eat _____ slices of pizza every second.

☐ Vocabulary Practice

A. Completion. Complete the information using words from the box. Two words are extra.

covered	ingredient	serving	traditional
developed	learned	step	various

Who made the first hamburger?

The hamburger is one of the best-loved foods in the world. In the U.S. alone, people eat more than 14 billion (14,000,000,000) burgers every year! But who made the first one? No one knows for certain, but there are **1.** _____ stories about where this favorite food comes from.

In the 1200s, Mongolian soldiers **2.** _____ to soften meat by placing it under the saddle[1] of their horses while riding. Then they ate the meat—without cooking it. It was the first kind of "meat patty." Hundreds of years later, people in the town of Hamburg, Germany, developed "Hamburg steak"—a dish of salty meat on round bread. They brought this **3.** _____ German food with them when they came to live in America in the 1900s.

The "hamburger" that we know today really started in the USA. In 1885, a man from Wisconsin named Charles Nagreen had the idea of **4.** _____ meatballs between pieces of bread. That way, people could eat them while walking. In the same year, a man in Hamburg, New York, sold sandwiches using pork as the main **5.** _____. One day, he did not have enough pork and decided to use beef. Without knowing it, he had **6.** _____ a new type of food—one that is now eaten by millions around the world.

[1] A **saddle** is a seat for a rider, usually made of leather (animal skin), which is placed on a horse's back.

▲ A monk at Shaolin temple in China carries a take-out burger meal. Today the hamburger is a global food. But where did the first burger come from?

B. Words in Context. Complete each sentence with the best answer.

1. If you are poor, you have _____ money.
   a. a lot of   b. only a little

2. If something is standard, it is _____.
   a. usual   b. not usual

3. A tradition is _____ way to do something.
   a. a new   b. an old

4. If you cover something, you put another thing _____ it.
   a. under   b. over

5. When something develops, it _____.
   a. changes   b. stays the same

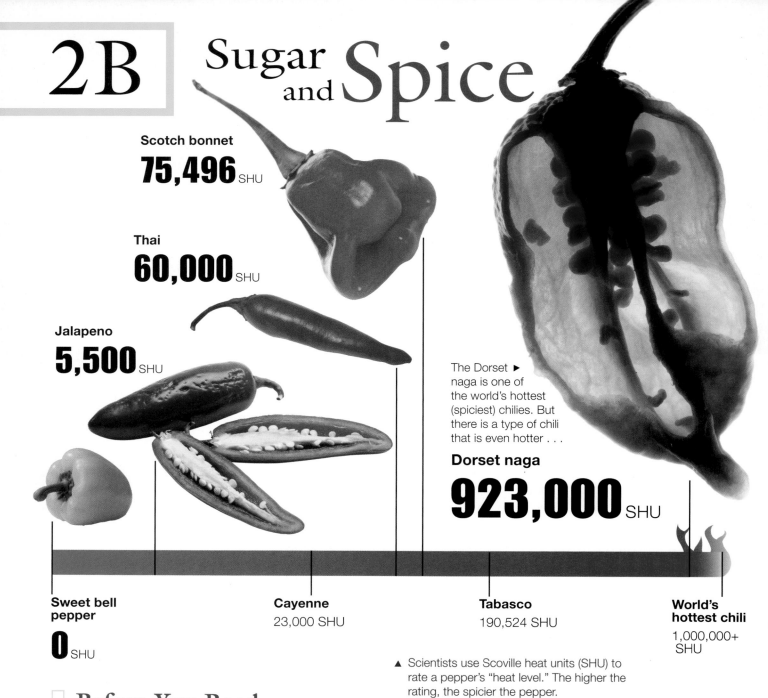

2B Sugar and Spice

Scotch bonnet
75,496 SHU

Thai
60,000 SHU

Jalapeno
5,500 SHU

The Dorset ▶ naga is one of the world's hottest (spiciest) chilies. But there is a type of chili that is even hotter . . .

Dorset naga
923,000 SHU

Sweet bell pepper
0 SHU

Cayenne
23,000 SHU

Tabasco
190,524 SHU

World's hottest chili
1,000,000+ SHU

▲ Scientists use Scoville heat units (SHU) to rate a pepper's "heat level." The higher the rating, the spicier the pepper.

☐ Before You Read

A. True or False. What do you know about chili peppers? Read the information above and answer true (**T**) or false (**F**).

1. The Dorset naga is the world's hottest chili.	T	F
2. The Scoville is a type of chili pepper.	T	F
3. Jalapeno peppers are hotter than Scotch bonnets.	T	F
4. Sweet bell peppers have a very low heat level.	T	F

B. Scan. Quickly scan the passage on the next page. What is the name of the world's spiciest chili pepper?

~The Hottest Chili~

1　You may have experienced the feeling—your mouth feels like it's on fire and the heat causes your eyes to water. You've just eaten one of nature's spiciest foods—the chili pepper!

5　Chili peppers, also called chilies, are found in various dishes around the world—from Indian curries to Thai tom yum soup to Mexican enchiladas. Chilies come from the capsicum plant, and they are "hot" because they contain an ingredient called capsaicin.

10　Eating a hot chili can be painful, but the capsaicin may be good for your health. It opens your nose so you can breathe better. It may even be good for losing weight: capsaicin makes you feel less hungry and makes your body use more calories.[1]

15　We can measure the capsaicin in chilies with Scoville heat units (SHU). A fairly spicy green pepper has about 1,500 units. The world's hottest chili, the Naga Jolokia ("Ghost Pepper"), has more than a million!

　　The Naga Jolokia is produced in the Assam region of
20　India. Recently, Anandita Dutta Tamuly, a 26-year-old mother from Assam, broke a world record by eating 51 of these hot peppers—in just two minutes!

　　"I found eating chilies was a great way to stay healthy," says Tamuly, who began eating chilies when she was a
25　child. "Every time I have a cold or flu I just munch[2] on some chilies and I feel better. To be honest,[3] I barely notice them now."

"Every time I have a cold or flu I just munch on some chilies and I feel better."

—Anandita Dutta Tamuly, world champion chili eater

Assam, India

[1] **Calories** are units used to measure the energy value of food.
[2] If you **munch** food, you eat it by chewing it slowly.
[3] If someone is **honest**, they say the truth.

Reading Comprehension

A. Multiple Choice. Choose the best answer for each question.

Gist **1.** What is the reading mainly about?
  a. how to measure the capsaicin in chilies
  b. dishes that are made with chilies
  c. interesting facts about chilies
  d. weight loss and chilies

Reference **2.** In line 2, the word *it* refers to _____.
  a. the feeling
  b. your mouth
  c. the chili pepper
  d. the heat

Detail **3.** How many SHU are in the Naga Jolokia chili?
  a. just over 50
  b. between 1,000 and 2,000
  c. a little less than 1,000,000
  d. over 1,000,000

Vocabulary **4.** In line 21, someone has a *world record* if they _____.
  a. eat more Naga Jolokia chilies than anyone else
  b. make a recording of someone eating Naga Jolokia chilies
  c. eat two or more Naga Jolokia chilies very quickly
  d. make the best-tasting dish using Naga Jolokia chilies

Paraphrase **5.** In lines 26–27, the phrase *I barely notice them now* could be replaced by _____.
  a. I really feel the heat of the chilies now
  b. I sometimes forget to eat chilies now
  c. I usually don't eat hot chilies now
  d. I almost don't feel the heat of the chilies now

B. True or False. According to the passage, are the sentences below true or false? Circle **T** (true), **F** (false), or **NG** (not given in the passage).

	T	F	NG
1. Capsaicin helps you breathe better.	T	F	NG
2. Capsaicin makes you feel happier.	T	F	NG
3. Capsaicin makes you feel hungrier.	T	F	NG
4. Capsaicin helps you fall asleep at night.	T	F	NG
5. Capsaicin makes chili peppers "hot."	T	F	NG

Vocabulary Practice

A. Matching. Read the information below and match each word in red with a definition.

Most of us have experienced the taste of sugar, but how many of us know where it comes from? The man in the picture is standing in front of a field of sugarcane, a plant which produces sugar. It only grows in hot countries like Brazil because it needs lots of water and sunlight. After they collect the plants, workers in factories break the long stalks to get the sweet juice out. Then they cook the juice in big pots. This causes the sugar to come out of the juice.

1. to cut into two or more pieces _____

2. to make something happen _____

3. to sense, feel, or be affected by (something) _____

4. to create or make (something) _____

5. a living thing that is green and grows in the ground _____

B. Completion. Complete the information using words from the box. One word is extra.

health	plant	recent	
measure	produce	stay	units

Chocolate comes from a **1.** _____ called the cacao tree. The tree grows mainly in Africa and Latin America. Cacao trees have fruit with beans inside. Workers pick the fruit and take the beans out to be dried, cooked, and turned into chocolate.

People from Switzerland eat the most chocolate in the world. In a **2.** _____ year, people in Switzerland ate about 10 kilograms (22 pounds) per person!

In some ways, eating sweet foods like chocolate can be good for your **3.** _____. But eating too many sweet products can cause problems. Sugar and chocolate have a lot of food energy. We can **4.** _____ this energy in **5.** _____ called calories. If you want to **6.** _____ fit, you need to be careful about how many calories you take in each day.

▲ Dried cacao beans in Polynesia are made ready for shipping to other countries.

Word Partnership

Use **break** with:
break **your leg** (or **arm**, etc.),
break **a record**, break **a rule**,
break **a promise**.

A Taste of Mexico

A. Preview. What do you know about Mexican food? What ingredients are used in Mexican dishes?

B. Summarize. Watch the video, *A Taste of Mexico*. Then complete the summary below using words from the box.

experience	standard
learning	stay
poor	step
recent	traditional
served	various

▲ Oaxaca is famous for its traditional dances, as well as its traditional food.

Many visitors travel to Oaxaca in Mexico to

1. _____ its culture. It may be a

2. _____ state, but it is rich in history and art.

Oaxaca is famous for its **3.** _____ dances and old

buildings, and most of all, its food. In **4.** _____

years, many foreigners have become interested in

5. _____ how to make Oaxacan food. They

6. _____ in Oaxaca for several months and go to

cooking school there.

The first **7.** _____ in Oaxacan cooking is making

mole. Mole is a sauce with chili peppers and

8. _____ spices. It is a **9.** _____

ingredient in many Oaxacan dishes, and is often

10. _____ with chicken, meat, and other foods.

C. Think About It.

1. Susanna Trilling says Oaxacan food is "very complex." In other words, it has many ingredients and traditions. Do you think that the best kinds of food are "complex"?

2. If you could go to a cooking school, what kind of cooking would you want to learn?

To learn more about Mexican food, visit elt.heinle.com/explorer

UNIT 3
That's Entertainment!

Movie star Johnny Weismuller, dressed as Tarzan, ▶ is photographed with Cheeta, a chimpanzee. Cheeta acted with Weismuller in several Tarzan movies in the 1930s.

Discuss these questions with a partner.

1. What are your favorite kinds of films?

2. What kinds of movies are popular in your country? Why are they popular?

3. Are there any famous movie-makers from your country? What kinds of films do they make?

29

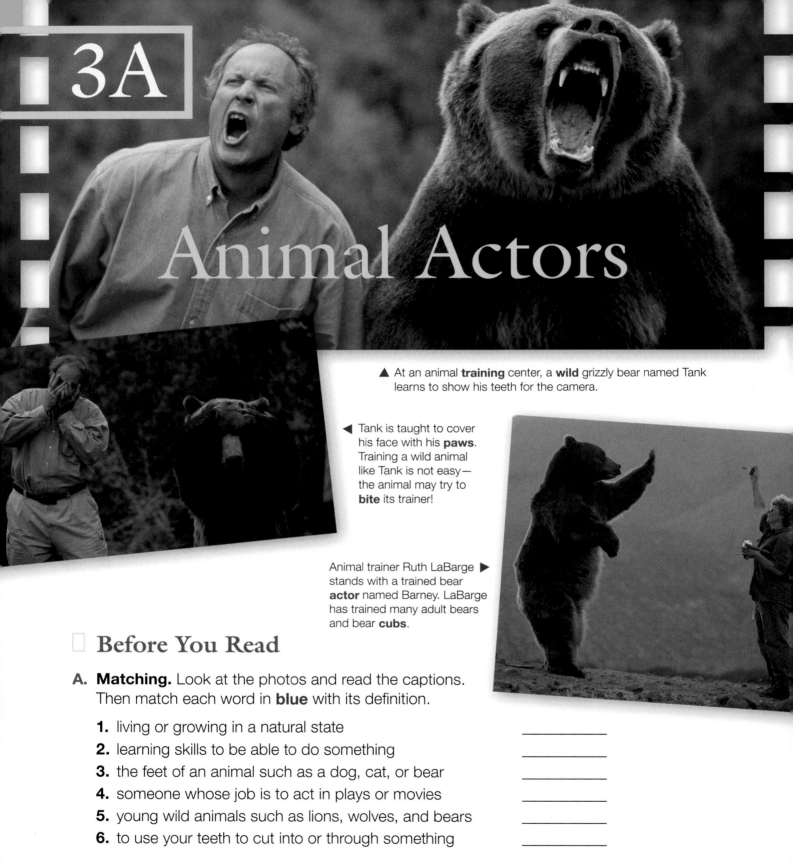

3A

Animal Actors

▲ At an animal **training** center, a **wild** grizzly bear named Tank learns to show his teeth for the camera.

◄ Tank is taught to cover his face with his **paws**. Training a wild animal like Tank is not easy—the animal may try to **bite** its trainer!

Animal trainer Ruth LaBarge ▶ stands with a trained bear **actor** named Barney. LaBarge has trained many adult bears and bear **cubs**.

☐ Before You Read

A. Matching. Look at the photos and read the captions. Then match each word in **blue** with its definition.

1. living or growing in a natural state _____
2. learning skills to be able to do something _____
3. the feet of an animal such as a dog, cat, or bear _____
4. someone whose job is to act in plays or movies _____
5. young wild animals such as lions, wolves, and bears _____
6. to use your teeth to cut into or through something _____

B. Scan. You are going to read about an unusual summer job. Quickly scan the reading to answer the questions below. Then read again to check your answers.

1. What was the young man's job?   2. Where did he work?

My GRIZZLY Summer Job

1   Russell Chadwick remembers the summer he turned 16—
it was the time he wrestled[1] with grizzly bears!

Russell's adventure started when he came to stay at Wasatch
Rocky Mountain Wildlife, an animal training center in
5   Utah. The center is run by Doug and Lynne Seus, who
train wild animals to be actors in television and movies.

Doug and Lynne asked high-school student Russell to help
them take care of two four-month-old grizzly bear cubs
called Little Bart and Honey Bump. That's more difficult
10   than it sounds, because even baby bears are pretty big.

Russell's job was to play with the bears to get them used
to humans. At the same time, he had to remember that
movie bears are still wild animals:

"One time Bump took a bite out of my back, and I had
15   to wrestle her to the ground. But it also showed me how
smart[2] she is. She knew she had done something wrong
and 'apologized'[3] by putting her head in my lap."[4]

Russell found that bears can understand more than just
"sit" and "stay." For example, when Russell called out
20   "Peekaboo!" to the adult bear, Tank, he covered his eyes
with his paws, just like a little kid.[5]

Although he didn't get a large fee for the job, Russell says
he values the experience more than money. When you've
wrestled with a grizzly bear, things like work and exams
25   don't seem so difficult anymore!

"One time Bump took a bite out of my back, and I had to wrestle her to the ground."

Heber City, Utah, U.S.A.

[1] If you **wrestle** with someone, you fight them by forcing them to the ground or into a painful position.
[2] Someone who is **smart** is very clever.
[3] If you **apologize** to someone, you say that you are sorry for hurting them or causing them trouble.
[4] Your **lap** is the front area formed by your thighs when you are sitting down.
[5] A **kid** is a child.

☐ Reading Comprehension

A. Multiple Choice. Choose the best answer for each question.

Gist

1. What is the reading mainly about?
  a. how to get a summer job in Utah
  b. what Russell did for his summer job
  c. why wild animals make good actors
  d. movies that the Seus's bears acted in

Vocabulary

2. In line 1, we could change the word *turned* to _____ .
  a. became
  b. grew up
  c. went around
  d. remembered

Detail

3. Which of these sentences is NOT true?
  a. Doug and Lynne Seus run Wasatch Rocky Mountain Wildlife.
  b. Doug and Lynne Seus work in Utah.
  c. Doug and Lynne Seus are animal trainers.
  d. Doug and Lynne Seus are movie actors.

Reference

4. In line 20, *he* refers to _____ .
  a. Russell   c. Tank
  b. Peekaboo   d. a little kid

Main Idea

5. What is the main idea of the last paragraph?
  a. Russell liked everything about the summer job except wrestling with the bears.
  b. Russell thinks that tests and homework are good ways to get ready for a summer job.
  c. Russell's summer experience helped prepare him for other things in his life.
  d. Russell didn't receive enough money for his summer job.

B. Summary. Complete the sentences below. Fill in each blank with no more than three words from the reading.

1. At Wasatch Rocky Mountain Wildlife, Doug and Lynne Seus train animals to work in _____ .
2. One summer, Doug and Lynne Seus asked Russell Chadwick to help them _____ two grizzly bear cubs.
3. Russell played with Little Bart and Honey Bump because the bears needed to _____ humans.
4. Russell thinks the job was a good experience even though he didn't get _____ .

Vocabulary Practice

A. Completion. Complete the information using words from the box. Three words are extra.

adult	fees	understanding
adventure	human	valuable
caring	job	
difficult	remember	

▲ A chimpanzee holds a chimp mask. Some trained chimps, such as Cheeta (page 29), have become famous movie stars.

Chimpanzees, or "chimps," can be trained to learn and
1. _____ various actions and movements. In this way, they can learn to "act" in films and on TV. About 200 chimps are now used in the U.S. entertainment business. Sometimes these chimps can seem almost like
2. _____ actors.

But some people are against training chimps to be actors. Although chimps are smart, they are still wild animals. At training centers, chimps may be hit if they don't do what the trainer says. Also, most TV and movie chimps are very young. "The chimpanzees we see used in entertainment are generally youngsters,"[1] says Dr. Jane Goodall, who runs a research center in Maryland, U.S.A., and has studied wild chimps in Africa. "Once they reach . . . six to eight years old, they become increasingly **3.** _____ to [control]."

Owners can charge high **4.** _____ for the use of their chimps in TV shows and movies. But once the chimps stop acting, they become less **5.** _____ to their owners. The cost of **6.** _____ for chimps is very high. Housing and food can cost up to $10,000 a year—and chimps can live for 60 years or more! Because of this, many older, **7.** _____ chimps spend the rest of their lives in cages[2] or are given to zoos.

[1] A **youngster** is a young person.
[2] A **cage** is a box, usually made of wire or metal, in which animals are kept so they cannot get away.

B. Definitions. Complete the sentences using the correct form of words in the box in **A**.

1. A(n) _____ is a kind of experience that is exciting and uncertain.
2. If something is _____, it is not easy.
3. A(n) _____ is money that you pay to do something.
4. If you _____ something, you think of it or keep it in your mind.
5. If something is _____, it is worth a lot of money.

Usage

We call people **humans** when we compare them to animals or machines:
Humans and animals communicate in different ways.
A computer can find answers to problems faster than a *human* can.

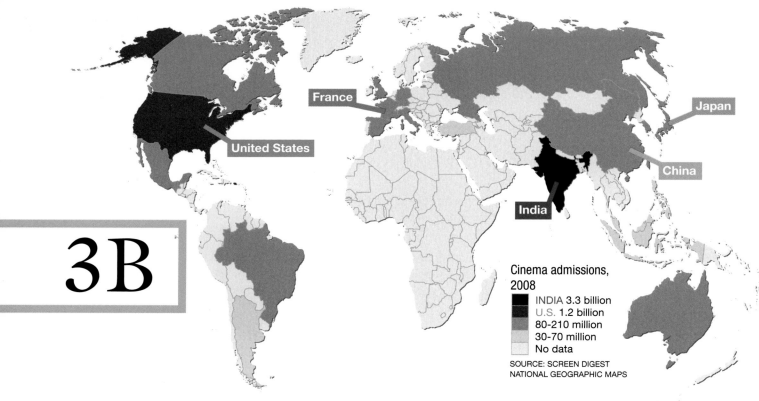

Cinema admissions, 2008
- INDIA 3.3 billion
- U.S. 1.2 billion
- 80-210 million
- 30-70 million
- No data

SOURCE: SCREEN DIGEST
NATIONAL GEOGRAPHIC MAPS

3B

Making Movies

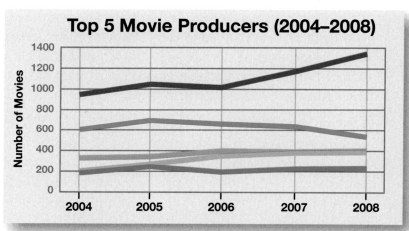

☐ Before You Read

A. Reading Maps and Charts.
Look at the map and chart. Then answer the questions below.

1. Which country had the highest number of cinema admissions (visits to movie theaters) in 2008? _____
2. Which country had just over a billion (1,000,000,000) cinema visits in 2008? _____
3. Which country's movie production went down between 2005 and 2008? _____
4. Which two countries produced about the same number of films in 2008? _____

B. Scan. Read the title and the first sentence of every paragraph on the next page. Check (✓) the things you think you'll read about. Then read the passage to check your predictions.

☐ what kinds of things you see in an anime movie
☐ how Hayao Miyazaki first started making movies
☐ why Hayao Miyazaki wanted to make movies

THE MASTER OF ANIME

"Is someone different at age 18 or 60? I believe one stays the same."

— *Hayao Miyazaki*

[1] A **robot** is a machine that can move and perform tasks on its own.
[2] If someone has **power**, they have a lot of control over people and activities.
[3] A **prize** is something that is given to the winner of a competition.
[4] Something that is **complex** has many different parts, and is difficult to understand.
[5] A **virtual** object or activity is something that is created by a computer to be like the real thing.
[6] If there is a **lack** of something, there is not enough of it or it does not exist at all.
[7] Your **imagination** is your ability to form new or exciting ideas.

Humans and robots[1] fight to save the world. Animals with magical powers[2] have great adventures. The world of *anime* is an exciting and colorful place. And who takes us there? Animators such as Japanese director Hayao Miyazaki.

Miyazaki started working in animation in 1963 and directed his first animated movie in 1979. More movies followed, including *Nausicaä of the Valley of the Wind*, produced in 1984. The following year Miyazaki started his own company, Studio Ghibli. Since then, the studio's films have won various prizes,[3] including an Academy Award in 2001 for *Spirited Away*.

Miyazaki's studio also produces *manga*, or comic books. *Nausicaä* began as a popular manga series set in the future. In the 1984 movie based on the series, Princess Nausicaä travels in a flying machine to study poisonous plants. It's just the beginning of a complex[4] and exciting story.

The director's films can be difficult to explain in just a few words. Nature and technology often play a central part in Miyazaki's stories. Understanding the way children see the world is also important to him. "I look at them and try to see things as they do," he says.

In his free time, Miyazaki stays away from television and other media. "Young people are surrounded by virtual[5] things," he says. "They lack[6] real experience of life and lose their imaginations."[7] Luckily for anime fans, Hayao Miyazaki hasn't lost any of his own.

☐ Reading Comprehension

A. Multiple Choice. Choose the best answer for each question.

Gist **1.** The passage is mainly about Hayao Miyazaki's _____.
  a. movie awards
  b. ideas about young people today
  c. animation company
  d. life as an animation director

Detail **2.** When did Miyazaki direct his first animated movie?
  a. 1963   c. 1984
  b. 1979   d. 2001

Vocabulary **3.** In line 20, the *movie based on the series* means that _____.
  a. the movie is part of a group of movies
  b. the ideas in the movie came from the *manga* comics
  c. the series tells us about things that happen in the future
  d. the movie was made before the *manga* books

Detail **4.** Which statement about Miyazaki's movies is NOT true?
  a. The stories are often about nature.
  b. The films are often about Miyazaki's children.
  c. The stories often include technology.
  d. The films can be difficult to explain in a simple way.

Inference **5.** Which of the following is probably true?
  a. Miyazaki believes children cannot understand complex stories.
  b. Miyazaki's *manga* have won more awards than his movies.
  c. Miyazaki has directed only a few movies since he started Studio Ghibli.
  d. Miyazaki thinks children should spend less time watching TV.

B. Sequencing. Number the events in time order from **1–5**. Then retell Miyazaki's life story to a partner.

_____ Miyazaki opens Studio Ghibli.

_____ Miyazaki wins an Academy Award for *Spirited Away*.

_____ Miyazaki begins working in animation.

_____ Miyazaki makes a movie version of *Nausicaä of the Valley of the Wind*.

_____ Miyazaki makes his first animated movie.

Vocabulary Practice

A. Completion. Complete the information using words from the box. Two words are extra.

director	following	including	series
explain	future	machines	
film	important	media	

James Cameron: Filmmaker

Date of birth: August 16, 1954
Place of birth: Ontario, Canada

- James Cameron is the **1.** _____ of some of the biggest movies ever, **2.** _____ *Aliens* (1986), *The Terminator* (1984), *Terminator 2: Judgment Day* (1991), and *Titanic* (1997).

- Cameron's *Terminator* movies are about a war between **3.** _____ and humans.

- Many newspaper writers and other people in the **4.** _____ thought Cameron's *Titanic* would not be a hit. In fact, it made $1.8 billion worldwide and became the biggest **5.** _____ of all time.

- **6.** _____ *Titanic*, Cameron took a break from making movies. In 2000, he produced a TV **7.** _____ called *Dark Angel*, starring Jessica Alba.

- Cameron's 2009 adventure movie *Avatar* was his first movie since *Titanic*. The story is set more than 100 years in the **8.** _____ on an alien world with islands in the sky. As in Hayao Miyazaki's films, nature and technology play a central part in the story.

"Filmmaking is about ideas, it's about images, it's about imagination, and it's about storytelling."

– James Cameron

B. Words in Context. Read the sentences and circle true (**T**) or false (**F**).

1. If you create something, you make something for the first time.	**T**	**F**
2. If you explain something to a group of people, you ask them how to do it.	**T**	**F**
3. The leader of a country has a very important job.	**T**	**F**
4. If a movie follows a TV program, it comes before that program.	**T**	**F**

Usage

We use **the media** to talk about all the ways that people get news and information:
*He told his story to **the media**.*

Media can take a singular or plural verb:
***The media** has/have changed people's ideas about the environment.*

History of Film

A. Preview. You will hear these words in the video. Use the words to complete the sentences.

camera	documentary	invented	screen	studio

1. People watch movies on a _____ in a movie theater.
2. The first movie technology was _____ more than a hundred years ago.
3. A company that makes movies is known as a movie _____.
4. Filmmakers use a _____ to shoot movies.
5. A _____ is a type of movie that is about real life.

B. Summarize. Watch the video, *History of Film*. Complete the summary below using words from the box. Two words are extra.

adventures	fee	future	including
directors	film	human	machine
explain	followed	important	series

For more than a hundred years, **1.** _____ has been one of the world's favorite kinds of entertainment. Movies let us experience **2.** _____ in faraway places and see things we have never seen before.

In the late 19th century, inventors produced a **3.** _____ called a kinetoscope. This showed a **4.** _____ of images very quickly. After paying a **5.** _____, people could look into the kinetoscope and watch the first kinds of movie.

The kinetoscope was soon **6.** _____ by the film projector. Projectors were used in the world's first movie theaters. Movies became more popular, and movie stars **7.** _____ Charlie Chaplin and Mary Pickford became famous worldwide.

Since those early days, **8.** _____ have used film technology to record **9.** _____ events around the world. In the **10.** _____, film technology will show us other ways to experience the world.

▲ Actors and crew shoot a scene for a movie in Mexico City in 1951.

C. Think About It.

1. How might movies change in the next 20 years? How about in the next 50 years?

2. What do you think has been the most important film in history? Why?

To learn more about entertainment, visit elt.heinle.com/explorer

A. Crossword. Use the definitions below to complete the missing words.

Across

1. to make by joining parts together
5. something used to make something else, usually food
7. to tell people that something has happened, e.g., in a newspaper
10. to describe something so it can be understood
12. all of something
13. If you _____ something, you place another thing over it.
15. not easy
17. happened only a short time ago
18. usual or normal
19. an exciting and/or dangerous event or experience

Down

2. picture
3. grown-up person
4. plan what something will look like
6. TV, radio, and newspapers are types of _____.
8. having little or no money
9. amount of money paid for a service
11. to make or create
13. to make something happen
14. movie
16. If you are _____ of something, you know it is true.

B. Notes Completion. Scan the information on pages **40–41** to complete the notes.

Field Notes

Site: Lines and Geoglyphs of Nasca and Pampas de Jumana
Location: Peru

Information:
- These mysterious lines and images are in the _____ of southern Peru.
- The designs, or "geoglyphs," are found over an area of nearly _____ km².
- Many lines are more than _____ years old and are so big that they can only be seen _____.
- The _____ people made most of the images, but no one is certain why.
- Some researchers think _____ was the main issue. The images were made for the _____, who they hoped would bring them rain.
- The lines were made by taking away the _____ on top of the ground and leaving the _____ underneath.

Mystery Lines

Sites: **Lines and Geoglyphs of Nasca and Pampas de Jumana**

Location: **Peru**

Category: **Cultural**

Status: **World Heritage Site since 1994**

Nasca Lines

Geoglyph Construction

PARACAS CULTURE		NASCA CULTURE		WARI CULTURE
800 B.C.	400	A.D. 1	400	800

In the **desert** of southern Peru, thousands of lines and images—including a spider, a monkey, and various other animals and plants—are drawn in the sand.

Who created these pictures, and for what purpose? Many of the images are more than 1,500 years old and can only be seen from the air. Because of this, some people thought they must have been made by visitors from space. Today, we know that most of the images were in fact created by people known as the Nasca. Less certain is why they were made.

A team of researchers in Nasca may have found an answer. "In this area, water was the **key issue**," says research director Markus Reindel. The Nasca lived in one of the driest areas in the world. Their river water came from the nearby Andes mountains. By making images for the mountain gods, the Nasca thought they would get more rainfall each year.

Over the years, however, the **climate** changed and the rivers ran dry. Sometime between A.D. 500 and 600, the last Nasca left the area. They left behind them one of the world's great mysteries.

Glossary

climate: the weather in a certain part of the world

desert: a dry, often sandy area of land with little rainfall

key issue: the main point or question

religious ceremony: a traditional event, or set of actions, relating to a god or gods

stage: the scene, or area, used for a certain

First seen from an airplane in the 1920s, the Nasca Lines have become one of the world's great mysteries.

Thousands of strange designs known as *geoglyphs* cover an area of nearly 4,000 km² (1,500 mi²), including the area shown right. The condor (a type of bird) is more than 120 meters (400 feet) long — about the length of a standard soccer field.

HERON
IGUANA
SPIRAL
LIZARD
SPIDER
FLOWER
TREE
HANDS
ALGA
PAN AMERICAN HIGHWAY
TRAPEZOID
CONDOR
FISH

CONDOR

The Nasca Lines were not all created at the same time, for the same purpose. The earliest designs were made by people known as the Paracas. These included images of 30-meter (100-foot) humans with large eyes: no one knows for certain what they were for. The Paracas were followed by the Nasca people. At first their pictures were mostly of the natural world. Later these developed into long lines and detailed patterns. According to researcher Markus Reindel, the later Nasca Lines "weren't meant as images to be seen anymore, but **stages** to be walked upon, to be used for **religious ceremonies**."

rope   pole

① ② ③

Creating the Nasca Lines

Scientists now think they understand how the drawings were made:

Step ① The Nasca placed large stones to mark the outer lines of the drawing.

Step ② The darker stones on top of the ground were taken away, leaving the lighter stones underneath.

Step ③ The darker stones were placed along the outer edges of the lines.

The Nasca also used simple technology—a pole and a rope—to make many circular designs.

A. Dictionary Skills. In English, there may be different meanings for the same word. Read the definitions for each word. Then write **1** or **2** next to the words in red below.

n. = noun   *v.* = verb

break (*v.*) **1.** to go against a rule, promise, or agreement **2.** to hit something until it
　　　　separates into two
center (*n.*) **1.** the middle of something **2.** a place where people take part in meetings/activities
plant (*v.*) **1.** to put seeds into the ground to grow **2.** to put something down firmly
serve (*v.*) **1.** to give people food and drinks **2.** to be used for a particular purpose
space (*n.*) **1.** an empty or available area **2.** the area beyond Earth where the stars and planets are
steps (*n.*) **1.** raised flat surfaces that you use to walk up or down **2.** a series of actions
　　　　taken with a certain purpose

1. At over 200 meters (650 feet) deep, Loch Ness certainly has enough space _____ to hold a monster.
2. Hundreds of years ago, people used to believe Earth was the center _____ of the universe.
3. The Scoville scale serves _____ as a good way to measure how hot something is.
4. The next step _____ for the Nausicaä manga series was to turn it into a movie.
5. People in Assam, India, plant _____ the world's hottest chili pepper.
6. Area 51 is "out of bounds," meaning you break _____ the law if you go inside.

B. Word Link. The suffix **–ly** changes adjectives (like *bad*) into adverbs (like *badly*). Read sentences **1–6** below. Then complete each sentence (**a–f**) with the adverb form of the word in red.

1. Early films were screened using a simple machine called a kinetoscope.
2. Many sweet foods are natural, like sugar and chocolate.
3. There are many people who believe ghosts are real.
4. A recent Hayao Miyazaki film is *Ponyo on a Cliff*, released in 2008.
5. The final cost of the movie *Avatar* was over US$300 million.

a. Honey is produced _____ by bees.
b. Now, anyone can make videos _____ by using their mobile phone.
c. No one knows for sure if Edinburgh castle is _____ haunted.
d. After 60 years, people _____ learned the truth about Nessie's photo.
e. Japanese animation has _____ become very popular in the West.

True Tales

Discuss these questions with a partner.

1. Do you know of anyone who has lived through a dangerous experience?

2. What are the most common news stories in your country?

3. Have you heard of anything so unusual that you thought it wasn't true?

▲ This watch was found on the *Titanic* wreck. Its owner was one of the 1,500 people who died when the ship sank in 1912.

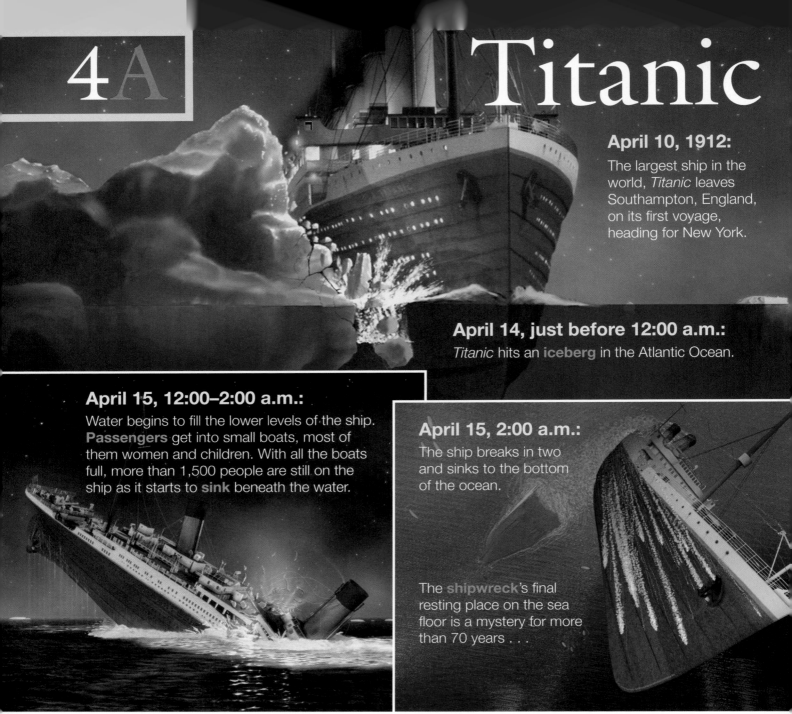

Titanic

April 10, 1912:
The largest ship in the world, *Titanic* leaves Southampton, England, on its first voyage, heading for New York.

April 14, just before 12:00 a.m.:
Titanic hits an iceberg in the Atlantic Ocean.

April 15, 12:00–2:00 a.m.:
Water begins to fill the lower levels of the ship. Passengers get into small boats, most of them women and children. With all the boats full, more than 1,500 people are still on the ship as it starts to sink beneath the water.

April 15, 2:00 a.m.:
The ship breaks in two and sinks to the bottom of the ocean.

The shipwreck's final resting place on the sea floor is a mystery for more than 70 years . . .

☐ Before You Read

A. True or False. Read the information above and circle True or False. Pay attention to the words in blue.

1. An iceberg caused Titanic to sink.	**True**	**False**
2. Over 1,500 passengers died when Titanic sank.	**True**	**False**
3. Nobody knew where Titanic's shipwreck was until the 1980s.	**True**	**False**

B. Scan. Read the title and the first sentence of each paragraph on the next page. How many times did Robert Ballard visit the *Titanic* shipwreck? Read the passage to check your answer.

"I've Found the TITANIC"

1 As a boy, Robert Ballard liked to read about shipwrecks—especially the *Titanic*. "My lifelong dream was to find this great ship," he says.

On August 31, 1985, Ballard's dream came true.
5 With video cameras and an underwater robot, Ballard found the two main parts of *Titanic* nearly four kilometers beneath the sea. He also saw many sad reminders[1] of *Titanic*'s end, including a child's pair of shoes lying on the ocean floor. There were more than
10 1,500 deaths that night in 1912.

Ballard reached the *Titanic* again in 1986 in a small submarine.[2] He used a deep-sea robot—a "swimming eyeball"—to take photos inside the ship. When they saw the images, other people wanted to visit the shipwreck.

15 When Ballard returned in 2004, he found the ship in worse condition. Other explorers had taken away about 6,000 items, including jewelry,[3] love letters, lamps, and even pieces of the ship. They believed the items should be moved to a safer place, but Ballard doesn't agree.

20 Ballard believes that taking things from *Titanic* is like robbing a grave.[4] Instead, he hopes to put lights and cameras on *Titanic*. With this technology, people can see the shipwreck on a computer and remember the great ship. "As long as she needs protection,"[5] says Ballard,
25 "*Titanic* will always be part of my life."

> "As long as she needs protection, *Titanic* will always be part of my life."
>
> —*Robert Ballard*

[1] Something that is a **reminder** of another thing makes you think about the other thing.
[2] A **submarine** is a type of ship that can travel both above and below the surface of the ocean.
[3] **Jewelry** refers to things made of gold, silver, or precious stones that people wear, such as rings or necklaces.
[4] A **grave** is a place where a dead person is buried.
[5] If something gives **protection** against something unpleasant, it prevents people or things from being harmed or damaged by it.

Reading Comprehension

A. Multiple Choice. Choose the best answer for each question.

Main Idea

1. What is the main idea of the reading?
   a. The story of the *Titanic* is very sad.
   b. Explorers who visit *Titanic* leave it in worse condition.
   c. Robert Ballard hopes more people will visit *Titanic*.
   d. The man who found *Titanic* now wants to protect it.

Detail

2. Which sentence about Ballard is true?
   a. Ballard read about the *Titanic* when he was a child.
   b. Ballard went inside *Titanic* to take pictures.
   c. Ballard believes pieces of *Titanic* should be taken to a safer place.
   d. Ballard's second visit was the last time he saw *Titanic*.

Paraphrase

3. The phrase *lifelong dream* (lines 2–3) is closest in meaning to _____.
   a. something you want to do at the end of your life
   b. something you want to do as a child
   c. something you want to do during the night
   d. something you have wanted to do your whole life

Detail

4. When was Ballard's second visit to *Titanic*?
   a. 1912   c. 1986
   b. 1985   d. 2004

Inference

5. Which statement would Ballard probably agree with?
   a. People should visit *Titanic* and see it for themselves.
   b. People should not remove things from *Titanic*.
   c. There should not be any lights or cameras on the *Titanic*.
   d. People should forget about *Titanic*.

B. Summary. Complete the sentences below. Fill in each blank with no more than three words from the reading.

1. Robert Ballard's _____ was to find *Titanic*, and in 1985, his _____ came true.

2. Ballard found the two _____ of *Titanic* at the bottom of the ocean.

3. One sad thing Ballard saw was a(n) _____ of shoes that used to belong to a child.

4. After Ballard visited the shipwreck, other explorers went there and _____ about 6,000 things.

5. Ballard doesn't think people should visit *Titanic*. He thinks the shipwreck needs _____.

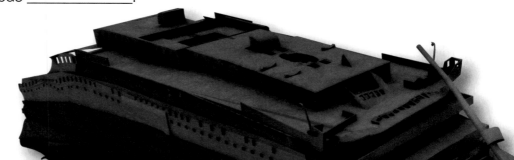

Vocabulary Practice

A. Completion. Complete the information using words from the box. Two words are extra.

believe	instead	reach
conditions	items	returned
deaths	main	

Why were there so many
1. _____ on the night that *Titanic* sank? One reason is that weather **2.** _____ were very bad. The accident happened in April when the air and water were very cold. Scientists **3.** _____ that most of the passengers who fell into the water died in less than 15 minutes. But the **4.** _____ reason for the high number of deaths is that there were not enough lifeboats. There were 2,223 people on the ship—but only enough boats for 1,186 people. Also, many people could not **5.** _____ the lifeboats in time before the boat broke apart. In the end, only 706 people **6.** _____ safely to land.

▲ At first, most people could not believe the news of *Titanic*'s sinking. The ship was designed to be unsinkable.

B. Words in Context. Complete each sentence with the best answer.

1. If you return, you go to a place _____.
   a. for the first time   b. again

2. If people agree, they have _____ about a subject.
   a. the same idea   b. different ideas

3. If you drink tea instead of coffee, you drink _____.
   a. tea   b. both tea and coffee

4. If you hope for something, you _____ that thing to happen.
   a. don't want   b. want

5. If you reach a place, you are _____ to get to that place.
   a. able   b. not able

Usage

If you **agree with** someone, you have the same idea or opinion as that person.

If you **agree to** do something, you say that you will do it.

4B Danger!

Average Number of Lightning Flashes (per sq. km/year)

■ More than 50	▨ 6–9	▨ 0.4–0.7
■ 30–50	□ 2–5	▨ 0.1–0.3
▨ 10–29	□ 0.8–1.9	□ Less than 0.1

Before You Read

A. Reading Maps. Use the map to answer the questions (**1–4**).

1. Lightning flashes happen most often **a.** over land **b.** over water.
2. Europe has the **a.** least **b.** most lightning flashes of any continent.
3. Central Africa has **a.** fewer **b.** more lightning flashes than central Asia.
4. Most of South America gets **a.** more **b.** less than 10 lightning flashes per km[1] per year.

¹ km = kilometer, a unit of length equal to 1,000 meters, or .62 miles

B. Scan. You are going to read about a boy who was struck by lightning. Quickly scan the reading to answer the questions below. Then read again to check your answers.

1. **Who** was hit?
2. **When** was he hit?
3. **Where** did it happen?
4. **What** was he doing?
5. **How** old was he?

"I Was Struck By LIGHTNING!"

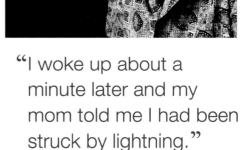

1   On a sunny afternoon in 2004, nine-year-old Geoff Banninger was walking to a park in Colorado to see his sister play softball. But before he got to the park, Geoff was struck[1] by lightning.

5   The lightning stopped Geoff's heart and his breathing. It burned his hair and left a burn line from his head to his foot. It blew his glasses off his face and melted[2] them. It even made a hole in the bottom of his shoe. "I woke up about a minute later," says Geoff, "and my
10   mom told me I had been struck by lightning."

  What is lightning? A lightning strike is the result of a buildup of electrical charges[3] inside a cloud. We usually see lightning during stormy weather. But, as Geoff discovered, it can happen even on a sunny day.

15   Geoff's legs felt strange after he was hit, but he hasn't had any further problems since then. "I'm a lucky guy," he says. But being lucky is not the only way to ensure your safety during a thunderstorm. You can also follow the 30/30 rule: if you see lightning, and then hear
20   thunder less than 30 seconds later, go inside a building. Then wait 30 minutes after the last thunder or lightning before you go back outside.

  So how likely is it you will be hit by lightning? Fortunately,[4] it's not a common problem. According to
25   the U.S. National Weather Service, your chance of being struck in your lifetime is only 1 in 5,000.

"I woke up about a minute later and my mom told me I had been struck by lightning."

—Geoff Banninger

Arvada, Colorado, U.S.A.

[1] If you are **struck** by something, it means you have been hit by it.
[2] When something **melts**, it changes from solid to liquid, usually because it has been heated.
[3] An electrical **charge** is an amount of electricity that is held in or carried by something.
[4] If someone or something is **fortunate**, they are lucky.

☐ Reading Comprehension

A. Multiple Choice. Choose the best answer for each question.

Detail
1. Which sentence about Geoff Banninger is NOT true?
a. The lightning stopped his breathing.
b. The lightning burned his hair.
c. The lightning left a line around his shoe.
d. The lightning stopped his heart.

Inference
2. Which of the following is probably true?
a. Geoff remembers being struck by lightning.
b. When Geoff was struck by lightning, his mother was nearby.
c. Geoff's sister saw him get hit.
d. Geoff believes he has a very unlucky life.

Reference
3. In line 14, the word *it* refers to _____.
a. stormy weather
b. cloudy weather
c. a lightning strike
d. a sunny day

Detail
4. According to the 30/30 rule, you should go inside a building _____.
a. when thunder and lightning are less than 30 seconds apart
b. at least 30 minutes after the last thunder or lightning
c. when you see lightning, but don't hear thunder
d. any time you hear thunder and see lightning

Main Idea
5. What is the main idea of the last paragraph?
a. Most people are never struck by lightning.
b. It's common to be struck by lightning.
c. It's fortunate if you are struck by lightning.
d. Lightning usually strikes in the afternoon or early evening.

B. Matching. What is the main idea of each paragraph in the reading?
Match each heading (**a–e**) with the correct paragraph.

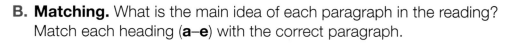

Paragraph		Heading
1. (from line 1)	_____	**a.** How to Stay Safe During a Thunderstorm
2. (from line 5)	_____	**b.** Will You Be Struck by Lightning?
3. (from line 11)	_____	**c.** The Day Geoff Banninger Was Struck by Lightning
4. (from line 15)	_____	**d.** Why Do We Have Lightning?
5. (from line 23)	_____	**e.** What Happened When Geoff Was Struck?

Vocabulary Practice

A. Matching. Read the information below and match each word in red with a definition.

TYPES OF  Sharks

The **whale shark** is the biggest fish in the ocean. It can grow as large as a bus. Its heart can weigh 20 kg (44 lb) or more!

The **hammerhead shark** uses its strangely shaped head to hold down food while eating. The chance of being attacked by a hammerhead is very small. Since 1580, there have only been 33 recorded attacks.

An **angel shark** hides at the bottom of the sea and waits for fish to come by. Then it opens its mouth and the fish swim in.

1. the possibility, or opportunity, for something to happen   _____

2. the part of an animal's body that pumps (pushes out) blood   _____

3. do nothing for a time until something happens   _____

B. Completion. Complete the information using words from the box. One word is extra.

common	ensure	further	happen	heart	likely	result	rule

What should you do in a shark attack? Eleven-year-old Aaron Perez knew the answer. One evening he was swimming in the Gulf of Mexico when a bull shark attacked him. There was one **1.** _____ Aaron knew about sharks: if a shark attacks you, you should hit it in the eye or the gills.[1] Aaron hit the shark hard with his hand, and it let him go. He got out of the water safely.

When they **2.** _____, shark attacks can be deadly. But they are not
3. _____. Each year, sharks usually kill fewer than ten people worldwide.
A **4.** _____ 100 people are attacked and injured. You are more
5. _____ to be attacked in parts of the sea where tourists throw in food to bring in sharks. The sharks learn to return to these places to find food.

However, people are dangerous to sharks, too. Every year, 60 million sharks are killed for food and medicine. As a **6.** _____ of this hunting, some species, or kinds, of sharks may die out completely. "Time is running out[2] for these species," says Sonja Fordham, a scientist at the Ocean Conservancy. "Programs to protect sharks [are] needed to
7. _____ that these magnificent[3] species survive."

[1] **Gills** are the parts of a fish's body that it breathes through.
[2] If you **run out** of something, you use all of it so there is nothing left.
[3] If something is **magnificent**, it is very great.

Word Partnership

Use **rule** with: **follow a** rule, **break a** rule, **make a** rule

Lightning

▲ Lightning is very hot—a flash can heat the air around it to temperatures hotter than the surface of the sun.

A. Preview. Read the sentences below and complete the definitions.

Flashes of lightning are very bright and last for about 0.2 seconds.
Clouds are made of many particles of water.
Thunder can be heard ten miles or more from a lightning strike.

1. A flash is a _____ light.
   a. short, quick   b. long, slow

2. A particle is a very _____ piece or amount of something.
   a. large   b. small

3. Thunder is the _____ produced by a lightning strike.
   a. sound   b. light.

B. Summarize. Watch the video, *Lightning*. Then complete the summary below with words from the box. Two words are extra.

agree	chance	conditions	ensure	mainly
believe	common	deaths	item	reach

Lightning is a **1.** _____ sight in many parts of the world.
Lightning storms **2.** _____ happen in the summer when
weather **3.** _____ are hot and wet. Inside a rain cloud,
particles move around and build up electrical charges. This creates
lightning. Lightning usually stays inside the cloud, but sometimes it is
able to **4.** _____ the ground. Not all scientists
5. _____ on why this happens.
In the U.S., people have a greater **6.** _____ of being killed
by lightning than by hurricanes or tornadoes. Every year, there are
about 100 **7.** _____ caused by lightning in the U.S. The
best way to **8.** _____ you are safe during a lightning storm
is to stay indoors. If you are outside, stay away from high places or
tall trees.

C. Think About It.

1. What is the most dangerous natural event in your country?

2. What are some ways you can stay safe from natural events like lightning?

To learn more about true tales, visit elt.heinle.com/explorer

UNIT 5

Outdoor Activities

Discuss these questions with a partner.

1. How much time do you usually spend outdoors? What do you do?

2. What kinds of outdoor activities are popular in your country? Why are they popular?

3. Do you think it is important for people to spend time outdoors? Why or why not?

▲ A man jumps on his mountain bike near Ha Ling Peak, Alberta, Canada.

53

5A Baseball

Before You Read

A. Labeling. Read the information below. Then label the picture above with the words in **blue**.

Baseball is played by two teams, with nine players on each team. A player called a **pitcher** throws a small round ball called a **baseball**. A player from the other team known as the **batter** tries to hit the ball with a stick called a **bat**. If he misses the ball, the person behind him (the **catcher**) catches the ball and throws it back. The **umpire** decides if the throw is good. Teams get points by running and touching areas on the ground called **bases**.

B. Scan. You are going to read about international baseball. Quickly scan the reading on the next page (including the captions) to answer the questions below. Then read again to check your answers.

1. What are some names of people mentioned in the passage?

2. What were those people's jobs?

BASEBALL GOES GLOBAL

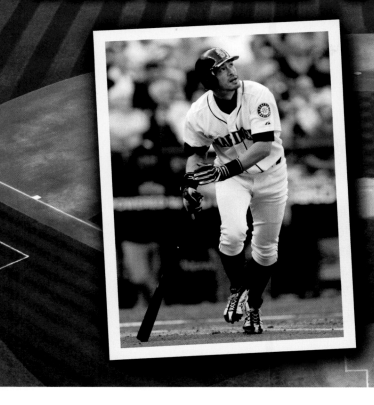

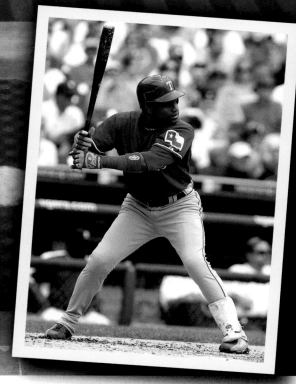

▲ Batters Ichiro Suzuki (left) from Japan, and Sammy Sosa from the Dominican Republic, both became successful foreign stars in the U.S. baseball league.

1   Baseball is sometimes called "the national pastime"[1] of the United States. But modern baseball is truly an international game.

Baseball began in the U.S. in the early 19th century. The first World Series was played in 1903. However, only American and
5   Canadian teams played in the series. The first non-U.S. victory[2] was by the Toronto Blue Jays in 1991.

Since the early 1990s, managers of U.S. teams have brought several foreign players to the U.S. game. Today, about 30 percent of players in American baseball come from foreign
10   countries, including Puerto Rico, Japan, South Korea, and the Dominican Republic.

One of the first Asian players in the U.S. was Japanese pitcher Hideo Nomo. Nomo got a lot of attention from the media when he joined the Los Angeles Dodgers in 1995. Soon, many other
15   U.S. teams were making contracts with players from other countries.

Today, world-class[3] baseball is available to more fans than ever before. In 1994, baseball became part of the Asian Games. In 2006, 16 teams from around the world took part in the first
20   World Baseball Classic—an international series of professional baseball games. Finally, baseball has become a truly global[4] pastime.

"For starting pitchers, we have two Dominicans, one Italian, one Mexican, and one Japanese."

—Tommy Lasorda, Los Angeles Dodgers manager, 1995

[1] A **pastime** is something you enjoy doing in your free time.
[2] A **victory** is success in a fight, war, or competition.
[3] Someone or something that is **world-class** is one of the best in the world.
[4] **Global** means concerning or including the whole world.

☐ Reading Comprehension

A. \Multiple Choice. Choose the best answer for each question.

Main Idea

1. Another title for the article could be _____.
- a. The History of the World Series
- b. Baseball: An International Sport
- c. The All-American Pastime
- d. Baseball Has a Good Year

Detail

2. In what year did Toronto win the World Series?
- a. 1903
- b. 1991
- c. 1994
- d. 1995

Sequence

3. Which of the following happened first?
- a. A non-U.S. team won the World Series for the first time.
- b. The first World Baseball Classic was held.
- c. Baseball was played in the Asian Games for the first time.
- d. Hideo Nomo started playing for the Dodgers.

Paraphrase

4. In line 19, the words *took part* could be replaced by _____.
- a. played
- b. learned
- c. left
- d. won

Detail

5. Which place is NOT mentioned in the article?
- a. South Korea
- b. Puerto Rico
- c. Venezuela
- d. Los Angeles

B. Completion. Complete the diagram below. Fill in each blank with one or two words from the reading.

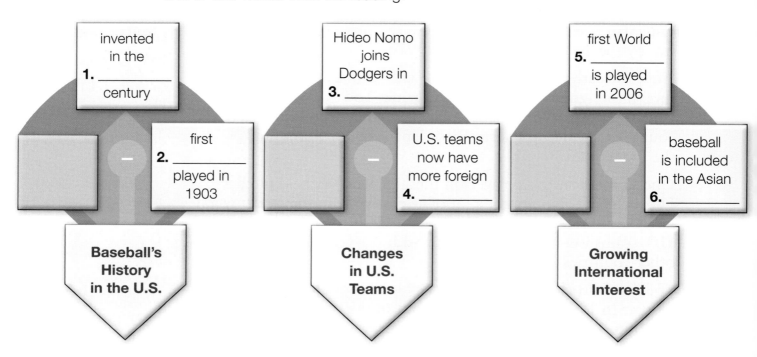

invented in the **1.** _____ century

first **2.** _____ played in 1903

Baseball's History in the U.S.

Hideo Nomo joins Dodgers in **3.** _____

U.S. teams now have more foreign **4.** _____

Changes in U.S. Teams

first World **5.** _____ is played in 2006

baseball is included in the Asian **6.** _____

Growing International Interest

Vocabulary Practice

A. Completion. Complete the information using words from the box. Two words are extra.

attention	join	several
available	manage	teams
contracts	percent	

Hours before a U.S. baseball game, players traditionally put mud on the baseballs. Why? Baseballs can be dangerous if pitchers are not able to hold them well. In 1920, a player was killed when a pitcher made a bad throw using a clean, new baseball. People tried
1. _____ different ways to make new baseballs easier to hold, but none worked well. Then, in 1938, a man named Lena Blackburne found an answer to the problem. Blackburne was a player for various U.S. baseball **2.** _____, including the Chicago White Sox and the Boston Braves, and later went on to **3.** _____ the

▲ Balls are rubbed with mud before every major league baseball game.

White Sox in the late 1920s. He found that using a certain type of mud from the Delaware River in New Jersey—together with a special "magic" ingredient—helped to make baseballs easier to hold. Blackburne's idea got a lot of **4.** _____ and many teams started using Lena Blackburne Baseball Rubbing Mud. Now, the company has **5.** _____ with all the major league baseball teams in the U.S. Since then, people have tried other ways, but they always go back to mud. After all, it works, and there's lots of mud **6.** _____!

B. Words in Context. Complete each sentence with the best answer.

1. If something is available, you _____ easily get it.
   a. can   b. can't

2. A person who can speak a foreign language can speak _____ one language.
   a. only   b. more than

3. If something is modern, it is _____.
   a. new   b. old

4. If you play in a team sport, you play it _____.
   a. on your own   b. with other people

5. If you join a club or event, you _____ it.
   a. leave   b. become part of

Word Link

We can add **–er** to some words to describe a person who does a certain action or job, e.g., *manager, teacher, writer, builder, researcher, designer, publisher, producer.*

5B

Outdoor Adventure

◀ Go **hiking** in beautiful Anmyeondo Recreational **Forest** in Taean Province.

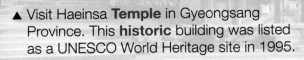

▲ Visit Haeinsa **Temple** in Gyeongsang Province. This **historic** building was listed as a UNESCO World Heritage site in 1995.

VISIT KOREA!

◀ Hike to the top of Bukhansan **Mountain** in the northern part of Seoul.

▲ Go rock **climbing** at Insubong.

☐ Before You Read

A. Matching. Look at the information above. Match the words in **blue** with the definitions (**1–6**).

1. _____ a large area where trees grow close together
2. _____ walking outdoors on rough ground
3. _____ moving toward the top
4. _____ important in the past
5. _____ high area of land with steep sides
6. _____ a building used to worship a god or gods

B. Scan. You are going to read about a hiking experience. Quickly scan the reading to answer the questions below. Then read again to check your answers.

1. Does the writer like hiking?
2. What was unusual about his hiking experience in Korea?

HIKING IN KOREA

1 **Travel writer Christopher Duffy hikes up a mountain—and gets a taste of Korean culture.**

On my first Saturday in South Korea, I decided to climb Mount Bukhansan. I enjoy hiking, and everyone told me about Bukhansan National Park. They mentioned
5 its beautiful forests, clean air, and historic temples. They didn't tell me about the huge crowds that go there every weekend!

Hiking is an activity that's generally done in groups in South Korea. After following the crowd for an hour,
10 I asked a group of hikers how far the summit[1] was. The leader of the group was Mr. Choi. When Mr. Choi saw I was alone, he said, "You will hike with us." Then he introduced me to his friends.

We hiked together for an hour until the group decided
15 to stop for lunch. I tried to get a sandwich from my backpack, but one of Mr. Choi's friends said, "No, no, no. You will eat with us." They provided a plate of pig's feet, some *kimchi*,[2] and a couple of drinks. After they shared their meal with me, the group decided they had walked
20 enough. They began walking back down the mountain.

I continued climbing, and finally arrived at the summit. A man standing on the mountaintop introduced himself as Mr. Kim. Together we shared a bottle of *makgeolli*, a traditional Korean drink, and admired[3] the view.
25 "In Korea," he said, "we say that the people you meet on the mountain are the best people." I thought about my day on Bukhansan, and I knew he was right.

▲ Bukhansan gets five million visitors every year—the highest number of visitors per square meter of any national park in the world.

Mt. Bukhansan, South Korea

[1] The **summit** of a mountain is the top of it.
[2] **Kimchi** is a traditional Korean dish made of vegetables.
[3] If you **admire** something (or someone), you like and respect it (or him/her).

☐ Reading Comprehension

A. Multiple Choice. Choose the best answer for each question.

Detail
1. People did NOT tell the writer about the _____ at Bukhansan.
    a. crowds
    b. temples
    c. forests
    d. clean air

Reference
2. The word *its* (line 5) refers to _____.
    a. South Korea's
    b. everyone's
    c. Bukhansan National Park's
    d. the crowd's

Vocabulary
3. The word *alone* (line 12) means _____.
    a. becoming tired
    b. not with other people
    c. very hungry
    d. from another country

Main Idea
4. What is the main idea of the last paragraph?
    a. It took a long time to get to the summit of Bukhansan.
    b. The author enjoyed hiking with other people on Bukhansan.
    c. The author tried makgeolli, a traditional Korean drink.
    d. The author probably won't return to Bukhansan.

Inference
5. What is probably true about the writer?
    a. In his home country, hiking is not usually done in big groups.
    b. In his home country, most people have heard of Bukhansan.
    c. He has been to Bukhansan a few times before.
    d. He felt the climb up Bukhansan was very difficult.

B. Sequencing. What is the main idea of each paragraph in the reading? Match each heading (**a–d**) with the correct paragraph.

Paragraph		Heading
1. (from line 2)	_____	**a.** Going to Bukhansan National Park
2. (from line 8)	_____	**b.** Words from a Man on a Mountaintop
3. (from line 14)	_____	**c.** A Meal on a Mountain
4. (from line 21)	_____	**d.** Meeting Mr. Choi and His Friends

Vocabulary Practice

A. Completion. Complete the information using words from the box. One word is extra.

activity	couple	general	leader	provide
arrive	enjoy	introduce	mention	

Hiking on Hawaii's Pu`u Kukui mountain is a very special leisure **1.** _____—one that very few people are able to **2.** _____.

If you **3.** _____ Hawaii to most people, they will most likely think of hotels and beaches with lots of tourists. Parts of Hawaii are, in **4.** _____, like that. But the western part of Maui, Hawaii's second largest island, is closed to tourists. It is a private scientific area owned by the Maui Land and Pineapple Company. Other than researchers and scientists, only 12 people can visit each year.

To get to hike on Pu`u Kukui, you first need to win a contest.[1] Then you take a helicopter ride to the private area. After hiking for a **5.** _____ of kilometers, you finally **6.** _____ at the top of Pu`u Kukui. From the mountaintop, you can see a magnificent view of forests, mountains, and sea.

Randy Bartlett is the **7.** _____ of the hikes in Pu`u Kukui. His job is to **8.** _____ hikers to the various unusual plants and to explain why each one is important. Many of the plants can be found nowhere else in the world. That's why so few people have the chance to experience this beautiful land.

[1] A **contest** is a competition or game.

▲ Many of the plants and trees in Maui's Pu`u Kukui Nature Reserve are found nowhere else on Earth.

B. Words in Context. Complete each sentence with the best answer.

1. If you share something, you use it _____.
   a. alone   b. together

2. If you enjoy hiking, you _____ going for a walk.
   a. like   b. don't like

3. When you arrive somewhere, you _____ the place.
   a. get to   b. leave

4. When you mention something, you _____ it.
   a. talk about   b. don't talk about

5. When you provide something, you _____ it.
   a. give   b. take

Usage

Use **enjoy** with the **–ing** form of the verb:
*I **enjoy** watch**ing** baseball.*
*My brother **enjoys** hik**ing**.*

EXPLORE MORE

Dubai World Cup

A. Preview. Read the information below. Then match each word in **blue** with a definition.

Horse racing is one of the world's most popular sports. One of the greatest racehorses of all time was Secretariat. In 1973, he ran the Kentucky Derby in less than two minutes, breaking the **track** record. In a later **competition**, he became the fastest racehorse ever by running at nearly 60 kph,[1] or 37.5 mph. (The fastest human **athlete** runs at about 43 kph, or 27 mph). Secretariat was part of a **stable** owned by Penny Chenery, one of the few female racehorse owners at that time.

[1] **kph** = kilometers per hour; **mph** = miles per hour

▲ The Kentucky Derby is one of the most famous—and oldest—horse races in the U.S. The race has been held every year since 1875. The world's richest horse race—the Dubai World Cup—is more recent; the first race was held in 1996.

1. a person who does a sport, such as running   _____
2. a group of racehorses owned by the same owner; also a building in which horses are kept   _____
3. an event in which people find out who is best at a certain activity   _____
4. a piece of ground that is used for races   _____

B. Summarize. Watch the video, *Dubai World Cup*. Then complete the summary below using words from the box. One word is extra.

Dubai, UAE

activity	available	including	provided
arrive	enjoy	manager	team
attention	foreign	modern	tradition

It's still dark, but there is already a lot of **1.** _____ on the race track in Dubai. Racehorses start to **2.** _____ as early as 5:00 A.M. They are getting ready for the Dubai World Cup.

In the morning, the **3.** _____ of the stable and his **4.** _____ of trainers work with the horses. The trainers give each horse a lot of care and **5.** _____. Each horse is **6.** _____ with special ice boots and is given a cool wash.

Horse racing is a very old **7.** _____ in Arabia, and many Arab people today still **8.** _____ watching horse races. During the Dubai World Cup, the large, **9.** _____ stadium[1] has many people, **10.** _____ both local and **11.** _____ horseracing fans.

[1] A **stadium** is a large sports field with seats all around it.

C. Think About It.

1. Do you believe it is OK to use animals in sports like horse racing?

2. What are the oldest sporting events in your country? Which provide the most money?

To learn more about outdoor activities, visit elt.heinle.com/explorer

UNIT 6

History and Legends

Discuss these questions with a partner.

1. Who were the first people in your country? Are there any stories or legends about them?

2. What stories or legends do you know from other countries?

3. Why do you think people like to listen to stories?

▲ A Native North American man holds up a gift to the gods.

6A Real-Life Legends

More than 200 years ago, Meriwether Lewis and William Clark led a group of European-Americans on an **expedition** to explore the western part of North America.

The group traveled from St. Louis to the Pacific Ocean. They **traded** with Native American people to get food, and they used a compass (right) to find their way.

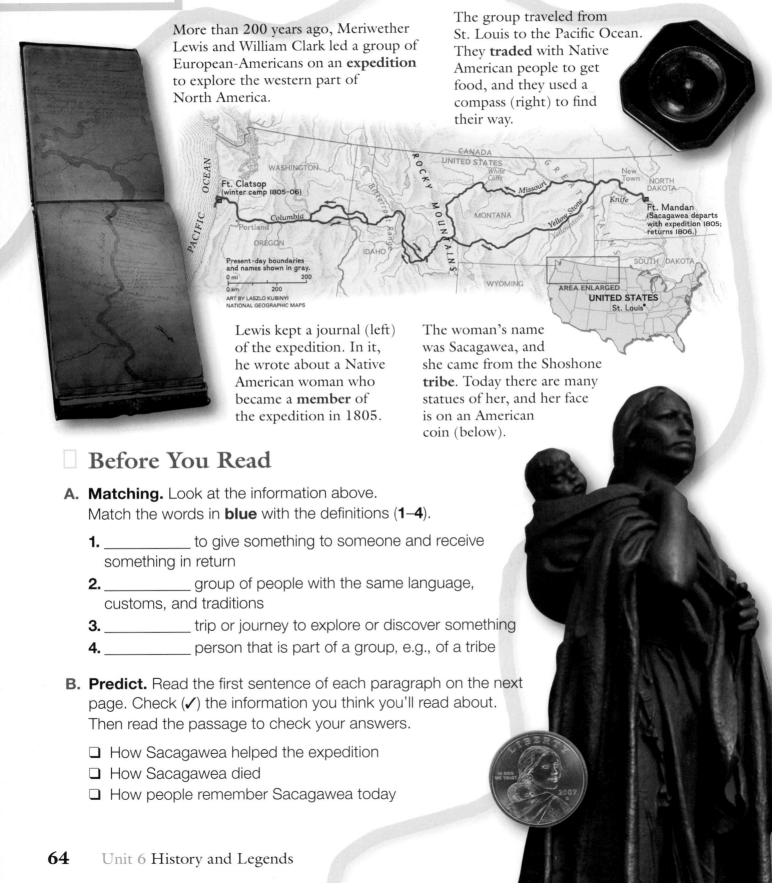

Lewis kept a journal (left) of the expedition. In it, he wrote about a Native American woman who became a **member** of the expedition in 1805.

The woman's name was Sacagawea, and she came from the Shoshone **tribe**. Today there are many statues of her, and her face is on an American coin (below).

☐ Before You Read

A. Matching. Look at the information above. Match the words in **blue** with the definitions (**1–4**).

1. _____ to give something to someone and receive something in return

2. _____ group of people with the same language, customs, and traditions

3. _____ trip or journey to explore or discover something

4. _____ person that is part of a group, e.g., of a tribe

B. Predict. Read the first sentence of each paragraph on the next page. Check (✓) the information you think you'll read about. Then read the passage to check your answers.

❑ How Sacagawea helped the expedition
❑ How Sacagawea died
❑ How people remember Sacagawea today

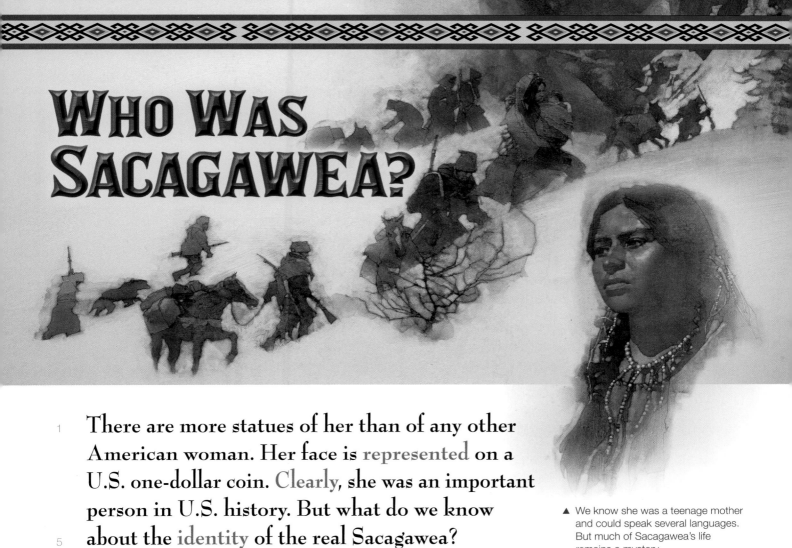

WHO WAS SACAGAWEA?

There are more statues of her than of any other American woman. Her face is represented on a U.S. one-dollar coin. Clearly, she was an important person in U.S. history. But what do we know about the identity of the real Sacagawea?

▲ We know she was a teenage mother and could speak several languages. But much of Sacagawea's life remains a mystery.

Sacagawea was part of a Native American tribe called the Shoshone. At the age of 11, she was taken away by the Hidatsa people. She was living among the Hidatsa when Meriwether Lewis and William Clark met her in 1804. Lewis and Clark were mapmakers. They were exploring the land in the west. Sacagawea spoke two different Native American languages, so they asked her to travel with them.

Sacagawea soon became an important member of the expedition. On May 14, 1805, a strong storm tipped over one of the boats. Sacagawea was able to reach many of the maps and other items in the water. Her quick actions saved important knowledge from being lost.

Sacagawea helped Lewis and Clark find a way across the mountains to the Pacific. She helped them make peace and trade with Native Americans. She also took care of her baby son.

Today, a Native American woman named Amy Mossett teaches people about Sacagawea's life. At the site of an old Hidatsa village, Mossett says, "This is where I feel closest to Sacagawea." Sacagawea died when she was about 25. Two hundred years later, she is remembered as an important woman in U.S. history.

☐ Reading Comprehension

A. Multiple Choice. Choose the best answer for each question.

Gist **1.** The reading is mainly about _____.
   a. why Sacagawea was able to speak several Native American languages
   b. why Sacagawea was an important woman in American history
   c. why Lewis and Clark went on an expedition to the west
   d. why Sacagawea left the Lewis and Clark expedition

Detail **2.** Which sentence about Sacagawea is NOT true?
   a. Sacagawea was part of the Shoshone tribe.
   b. Sacagawea lived with the Hidatsa tribe after she turned 11.
   c. Sacagawea asked Lewis and Clark to take her on the expedition.
   d. Sacagawea took her child with her on the expedition.

Detail **3.** Which person was NOT part of the expedition?
   a. Sacagawea   c. William Clark
   b. Meriwether Lewis   d. Amy Mossett

Vocabulary **4.** The word *tipped* (line 12) could be replaced with _____.
   a. looked   c. kept
   b. opened   d. turned

Paraphrase **5.** The phrase *I feel closest to Sacagawea* (line 20) is closest in meaning to _____.
   a. I can see Sacagawea   c. I look like Sacagawea
   b. I talk about Sacagawea   d. I understand Sacagawea

B. Sequencing. Match the phrases (**a–f**) to the events on the timeline.

> **a.** is taken from her people   **d.** lives as a member of the Shoshone
> **b.** dies aged about 25   **e.** meets Lewis and Clark
> **c.** saves maps and other items **f.** reaches the Pacific.

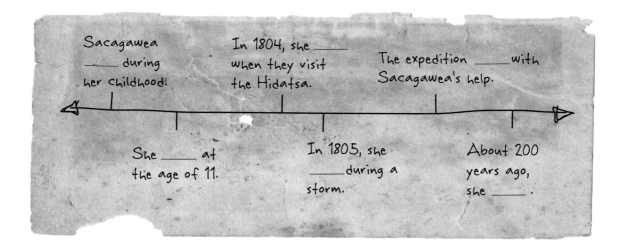

Sacagawea _____ during her childhood.

In 1804, she _____ when they visit the Hidatsa.

The expedition _____ with Sacagawea's help.

She _____ at the age of 11.

In 1805, she _____ during a storm.

About 200 years ago, she _____ .

Vocabulary Practice

A. Completion. Complete the information with words from the box.

knowledge	represented	strong
land	site	village

▲ As ruler of a strong Egypt, Hatshepsut was given gifts from many foreign lands.

THE WOMAN WHO WAS KING

On the west side of Egypt's Nile River is a small ancient
1. _____ where thousands of workmen once
lived. These were the people who helped build the tombs[1]
of Egypt's leaders. Nearby is the **2.** _____ of one
of Egypt's most magnificent buildings—the temple of Hatshepsut,
Egypt's greatest female leader.

There are many stories and legends about Hatshepsut, but much of her life is a mystery. "Nobody can
know what she was like," says Catharine Roehrig, author of *Hatshepsut: From Queen to Pharaoh*. But from
the historical records, we do know that Hatshepsut was a **3.** _____ leader. "She ruled for 20
years because she was capable[2] of making things work," says Roehrig.

Much of our **4.** _____ of Hatshepsut comes from statues and images created 3,500 years ago.
In many of these, she is **5.** _____ as a man wearing male clothing and a false beard.[3] It seems
that, although Hatshepsut was a woman, she ruled the **6.** _____ of Egypt as a king.

[1] A **tomb** is a place where the body of a person is placed after death.
[2] If someone is **capable** of something, like a job or activity, they are able to do it.
[3] A man's **beard** is the hair growing on the lower part of his face.

B. Completion. Complete the information with words from the box. One word is extra.

among	clearly	different	identity	knowledge	land

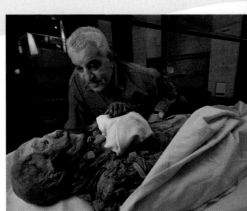

▲ Archeologist Zahi Hawass gets a close look at the mummy of Hatshepsut.

MYSTERY OF THE MISSING MUMMY

For years, archeologists had no **1.** _____ of what happened to
Hatshepsut after her death. When archeologist Howard Carter found
Hatshepsut's tomb in 1902, he discovered many of the queen's items,
but her body (or "mummy") was missing. What happened to it?

More than 80 years later, the question was answered. In 1989, archeologists
began studying a(n) **2.** _____ tomb called KV60, which was close to
Hatshepsut's. The body of a woman was found in the tomb, but no one was sure
of her **3.** _____. In 2006, archeologist Dr. Zahi Hawass decided to
send the mummy for a CT scan. The scan showed the woman was missing a
tooth. In Hatshepsut's tomb, a tooth had been found inside a royal box.
The royal tooth was a close match for the mystery woman's missing tooth.

The study showed that the woman was **4.** _____ the lost queen.
According to Dr. Hawass, the discovery of Hatshepsut's mummy is
5. _____ the most important finds in the history of Egypt.

> ### Usage
> A **town** is bigger than a **village**. A **city** is bigger than a town.
> *About 90 people live in that **village**. My **town** has 7,000 people. Tokyo is the world's biggest **city**.*

6B

Stories and Myths

☐ Before You Read

A. Labeling. Read the information below. Then label the pictures with the words in **blue**.

The Aborigines are a group of people who first came to Australia more than 40,000 years ago. They believe in the Dreamtime, or Dreaming, a "time before time" when great spirits[1] walked the earth and created all living things. The Aborigines are great storytellers and artists. Their cave paintings go back more than 6,000 years and are some of the oldest art in the world.

Many Dreamtime stories are connected with nature. The stories often include animals like the **frog, lizard, kangaroo, eel**, a bird called a **kookaburra**, and a small bear-like animal called a **wombat**. The passage on the next page is about one such story.

[1] A **spirit** is a ghost or supernatural being.

B. Scan. Quickly scan the passage on the next page. In what order do the animals appear in the story? Order them (**1–6**).

__ eel   __ frog   __ kangaroo   __ kookaburra   __ lizard   __ wombat

A TALE OF THE DREAMTIME

▲ An Aborigine man stands next to traditional Aboriginal rock art in Kakadu National Park, Australia. Aboriginal rock art often included animals from Dreamtime myths, such as the kangaroo (below).

1 One day, Tiddalik the frog was very thirsty. He drank the water in the rivers. Then he drank the water in the lakes. He drank and drank, and soon, all the water in the world was gone! The land was dry and brown, and the plants were dying.

5 The other animals were thirsty, too. They looked for water, but all the water was inside Tiddalik. The animals had a meeting and discussed the problem among themselves. The wombat had an idea. They would make Tiddalik laugh, and then all the water would come out of the frog's mouth. The animals agreed.
10 What else could they do?

First the kookaburra told Tiddalik funny stories, but the frog did not laugh. Next the kangaroo jumped up and down. The frog watched patiently, but he still did not laugh. Then the lizard walked in circles. He stood on two legs. He tried
15 everything to make the frog laugh. But Tiddalik didn't laugh. In fact, he was bored.

Then the eel began to dance. He turned his body this way and that way. Tiddalik smiled. Then the eel rose up on his tail. But eels live in the water, so normally they do not stand up.
20 The eel fell to the ground, and Tiddalik began to laugh. He laughed so hard that a flood of water came out of his mouth. The lakes and rivers filled with water. The land was green, the plants were healthy, and the animals were happy again.

Australia

Reading Comprehension

A. Multiple Choice. Choose the best answer for each question.

Gist **1.** The reading is mainly about _____.
- a. why Tiddalik drank all the water in the world
- b. how the wombat thought of a good idea
- c. how the animals made Tiddalik return the world's water
- d. why the eel was funnier than the other animals

Main Idea **2.** What is the main idea of the third paragraph?
- a. The lizard could not make Tiddalik laugh.
- b. Tiddalik was patient, but did not like to laugh very much.
- c. Most of the animals could not make Tiddalik laugh.
- d. The kookaburra's stories were not very funny to Tiddalik.

Paraphrase **3.** In lines 17–18, *turned his body this way and that way* means _____.
- a. he was swimming
- b. he was dancing
- c. he was smiling
- d. he was laughing

Vocabulary **4.** In line 21, the word *hard* could be replaced by _____.
- a. much
- b. fast
- c. tough
- d. difficult

Detail **5.** Which animal was able to make Tiddalik laugh?
- a. the kangaroo
- b. the wombat
- c. the lizard
- d. the eel

B. Sequencing. Number the events in order from **1–7**. Then retell the story of Tiddalik to a partner.

a. _____ The animals had a meeting to talk about the drought.

b. _____ The land was green again.

c. _____ Tiddalik the frog drank all the water in the world.

d. _____ The animals tried to make Tiddalik laugh.

e. _____ The land became dry and brown.

f. _____ Tiddalik the frog laughed hard.

g. _____ The water came out of Tiddalik's mouth.

Vocabulary Practice

A. Completion. Complete the information using words from the box. Two words are extra.

bored	else	idea	normally	rise
discussing	flood	meeting	patiently	thirsty

AESOP WAS A FAMOUS STORYTELLER IN ANCIENT GREECE. THIS IS ONE OF HIS STORIES:

One day, the Body Parts decided to hold a(n)
1. _____. They were unhappy that they did all the work while the Stomach got all the food. After
2. _____ the problem, one of them had a(n)
3. _____. "Why don't we just stop working?" it said.

So the Hands didn't pick up the food, the Mouth didn't take in the food, and the Teeth didn't chew the food. The Stomach waited **4.** _____. After a few days, the other body parts felt terrible. The Hands had nothing to do, so they were **5.** _____. The Mouth was very
6. _____ as it had no water, and the Legs were so tired that they couldn't walk. They didn't know what
7. _____ they could do, so they started working
8. _____ again.

▲ Aesop (620–560 B.C.) wrote several famous stories, or fables, including "The Tortoise and the Hare."

They learned that even the Stomach was important in its own quiet way, and everyone must work together, or the Body will fall to pieces.

B. Words in Context. Complete each sentence with the best answer.

1. If something is normal, it is _____.
   a. usual   b. unusual

2. If people discuss something, they _____ about it.
   a. talk   b. think

3. If something rises, it goes _____.
   a. down   b. up

4. The opposite of bored is _____.
   a. tired   b. interested

5. A flood of water means that there is _____ water.
   a. a lot of   b. a little

Word Partnership

Use **meeting** with: **have a** meeting, **go to a** meeting, **plan a** meeting, **attend a** meeting.

EXPLORE MORE

Native Americans

A. Preview. Read the information. What do you know about the native people of America?

When the first Europeans arrived in North America, they found about one million Native Americans already living there. The colors on this map represent the different language groups at that time. Several words from Native American languages are now part of the English language.

B. Summarize. Watch the video, *Native Americans*. Then complete the summary below using words from the box. Two words are extra.

Speakers of **Wakashan** include the Kwakiutl (*kwa-kee-oo-tl*) people. Traditional ceremonies are still performed by the Kwakiutl today.

Uto-Aztecan includes more than 30 languages, still spoken by over a million people from Oregon to Central America. English words taken from Uto-Aztecan include *tomato* and *coyote*. Sacagawea's people, the Shoshone, are part of this language group.

The **Eyak-Athabaskan** language group includes Navajo, the most widely used native language in the U.S. today.

Arawakan languages, spoken in northern South America and the Caribbean, provided English with words like *canoe*, *hurricane*, and *barbecue*.

among	else	land	represent	strong
different	joined	meeting	sites	villages

The first Native Americans arrived in North America about 30,000 years ago. They quickly moved out across their new **1.** _____. Over time, they became many **2.** _____ tribes, each with its own way of life. Some tribes lived **3.** _____ the buffalo on wide, open areas and lived by hunting; others made boats and lived by fishing.

But everything changed when the first settlers arrived from Europe. The settlers attacked the **4.** _____ in which the Native Americans lived. The native people tried to fight back, but the foreigners were too **5.** _____. In the end, there was nothing **6.** _____ that the Native Americans could do. They were made to leave their homes and live on **7.** _____ called reservations.

In the United States today, about 550 groups **8.** _____ the various native tribes. The purpose of these groups is to keep alive traditional ways of life and to create a better future for the Native American people.

C. Think About It.

1. Who were the first people in your country? Can you still see their culture today?

2. Do you know any other English words that come from other languages? Are there any words in your own language that come from other languages?

To learn more about history and legends, visit elt.heinle.com/explorer

Use the definitions below to complete the missing words.

Across

4. person who heads or guides the group
5. who you are
6. If something has a _____ of happening, it is possible it will happen.
8. to go back to the place you were before
9. usual and ordinary
11. not the same as others
17. If something is _____, it is found in large numbers or happens often.
19. a group of houses in a country area

Down

1. to arrive somewhere
2. to talk about something to reach a decision
3. to make sure
6. two; a few
7. from another country
10. something that happens because of another thing
12. a large amount of water covering a dry area
13. to get up
14. feeling in need of water
15. to become part of a group
16. If you _____ to do something, you say that you will do it.
18. relating to the time we are in

B. Notes Completion. Scan the information on pages **74–75** to complete the notes.

Field Notes

Site: Uluru-Kata Tjuta National Park

Location: _____, Australia

Information:
- Uluru is not a mountain, but a big _____.
  It is a symbol of _____ for Australians.
- The land became a national park in _____. It is both a(n) _____ and a(n) _____ heritage site.
- The explorer William Gosse gave it the name _____.
- The land was returned to the Aborigines in _____. The Aborigine word Uluru means "_____," or "Great Stone."
- The Anangu Aborigines have lived in the desert around Uluru for over _____ years. There are only _____ of them living there now.
- The Anangu never walk on Uluru as it is a(n) _____ for them.
- More than _____ tourists visit Uluru every year.

Rock of Legends

Site: **Uluru-Kata Tjuta National Park** (Ayers Rock)

Location: **Northern Territory, Australia**

Category: **Natural and Cultural**

Status: **World Heritage Site since 1987**

Uluru-Kata Tjuta National Park, Australia

Uluru changes color at different times of the day: it can be gray, brown, red, orange, or yellow—and sometimes purple, when it rains.

◄ Uluru is close to the very center of Australia, about 450 km (280 mi) by road from the closest town.

For scientists, it's the biggest rock in the world. For tourists, it's a center for outdoor adventure. For Australians, it's a **symbol** of national identity. For Aboriginal people, it's a traditional **holy** place. For everyone who comes to this special place, Uluru has a different meaning.

From far away, Uluru looks like a mountain, but it's really one big rock in the middle of a desert, 348 meters (1,142 feet) tall. An explorer named William Gosse made the first map of the area in 1873. He named it Ayers Rock, for the **prime minister** of Australia. The first **tourists** started arriving in the mid-1930s, and in 1958, the land became a national park.

Uluru is one of the few places in the world that is both a Natural and a Cultural World Heritage Site. There are Aboriginal rock paintings on its sides, and many Aboriginal stories about its history and **origin**. In 1985, the government gave the land back to the Anangu Aborigines, and changed the name back to the Aborigine word Uluru, meaning "Great Pebble" (or "Great Stone").

Glossary

holy: connected with God or religion
law: a rule agreed upon by a group of people or society
origin: beginning of something
prime minister: the head of a government
symbol: an object or sign that represents another thing
tourist: a traveler

At Home in the Desert

The land around Uluru is home to the Anangu Aborigine people. The Anangu have lived in the Australian desert for more than 20,000 years, but today there are only about 4,000 left. In the past, they lived by catching animals and finding desert plants. Now they live in small villages, but they still speak their traditional language, called Pitjantjatjara. About 20% of them can speak English.

▲ There are more than 400 groups of Aboriginal peoples in Australia, with many different languages and traditions.

The climb up the rock is ▶ not easy, as temperatures often reach 40 degrees Celsius (104 degrees Fahrenheit) or more. More than 30 people have died climbing Uluru.

Should Visitors Climb Uluru?

The Anangu never walk on Uluru, because for them, it is a holy place. They ask visitors not to climb on the rock. But every year, more than 500,000 tourists come to Uluru, and about a third of them climb to the top. Some people believe there should be a **law** against climbing the rock. But tourists spend $75 million there every year, so there is no simple answer to the problem.

A. Dictionary Skills. Some English words can be used as different parts of speech, such as noun (**n**), verb (**v**), or adjective (**adj**). Use the dictionary entries to mark the part of speech (**n**, **v**, or **adj**) for each word below (**1–6**).

> | *n.* = noun | *v.* = verb | *adj.* = adjective |
> | --- | --- | --- |
>
> **air**   *n.* the gas that we breathe *v.* to let air into a room or building
> **clear**   *adj.* obvious, easy to see *v.* to put things away
> **land**   *n.* an area of ground *v.* to arrive after traveling
> **plain**   *n.* a wide area of flat land *adj.* simple or easy to understand
> **share**   *n.* a part of something *v.* to use something together
> **work**   *n.* a job *v.* to do a job

How fast can you fly from France to England? In 2008, "Jet Man" Yves Rossy made the trip in only 13 minutes. He designed and used a special jet wing. With the jet wing on his back, he jumped from a plane 2,500 meters (8,200 feet) in the **1.** air (_____). Rossy had to be very careful as it was **2.** clear (_____) that the jet wing couldn't **3.** land (_____) on water, but he came down safely on a **4.** plain (_____) near the city of Dover. He **5.** worked (_____) on the jet wing for more than 15 years, and people from several countries **6.** shared (_____) ideas with him.

B. Word Link. The suffixes **–er** and **–or** change a verb into a noun for a person who does these things. Complete the sentences with the –er or –or noun of a verb in the box. Use your dictionary to help you.

> | design | direct | lead | manage | report | research |
> | --- | --- | --- | --- | --- | --- |

1. The _____ of a big football team usually gets a lot of money.

2. It takes a long time for a science _____ to finish a project.

3. A good _____ must make sure his/her product looks good and is easy to use.

4. Steven Spielberg is a famous _____ who has done many movies.

5. The _____ of a country has to make very big decisions.

6. A _____ must check that facts are correct before publishing a story.

▲ "Jet Man" Yves Rossy has reached speeds of over 300 kph (190 mph).

UNIT 7
Mind's Eye

WARM UP

Discuss these questions with a partner.

1. What kind of dreams do you often have?

2. Do you think dreams have meanings? What are some examples?

3. What do you think it means when someone says *your mind is playing tricks on you*?

◄ A man walks by an unusual piece of art in Paris, France.

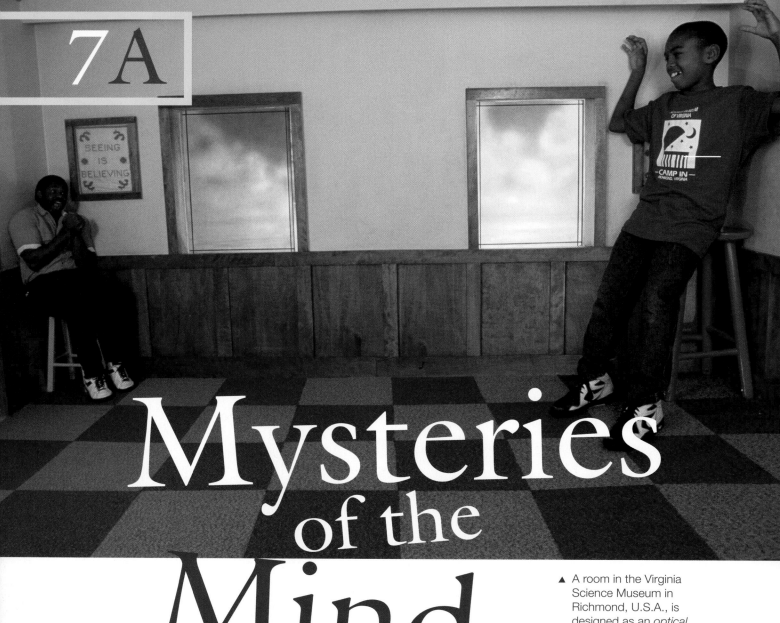

7A

Mysteries of the Mind

▲ A room in the Virginia Science Museum in Richmond, U.S.A., is designed as an *optical illusion*—something that is not what it seems.

Before You Read

A. Discussion. Look at the picture above. Then answer the questions below.

1. What is unusual about this picture?
2. How can you explain what you see?

B. Predict. Look at the title and the pictures on the next page. What is unusual, or "impossible," about each picture? What do you think causes it? Read the passage to check your ideas.

Seeing the
IMPOSSIBLE

1 Can you believe everything you see? Not always! You may see something one way, and then find out[1] you were wrong. You might even "see" something that isn't there at all. Errors like these are called *optical illusions*. *Optical* means related to sight, or vision—the way we see things with our eyes. An *illusion* is something that is not what we think it is.

5 Vision is also a personal thing. You may not see things in the same way as someone else. Look at these optical illusions, and compare what you see with your classmates. Do you see the same things?

1. Which red dot is larger?

Most people say it's the dot on the left. Now measure
10 the dots. They're the same size. The red dot on the left seems larger in relation to the blue dots around it.

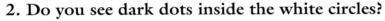

2. Do you see dark dots inside the white circles?

They're not really there. The difference between the dark squares and the white circles confuses[2] your brain. Therefore, your brain
15 *thinks* you see the dark dots.

3. Look at this picture of a vase. Can you see the faces?

Look again! Your mind has to choose the correct image, so it keeps changing
20 between the vase and the faces.

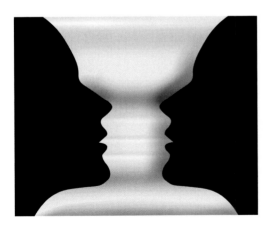

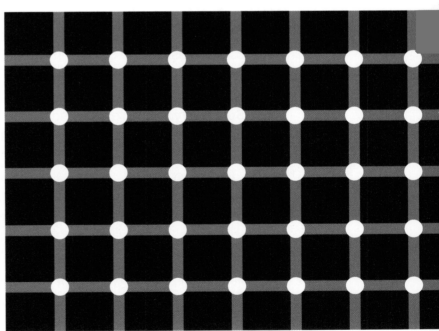

Vision is not always straightforward. Sometimes, your eyes see something, and your mind understands it easily. At other times, you may need to look twice. When this happens, you may be seeing an optical illusion.

[1] If you **find out** something, you learn about it.
[2] If you **confuse** two things, you get them mixed up.

☐ Reading Comprehension

A. Multiple Choice. Choose the best answer for each question.

Main Idea **1.** What is the main idea of the first paragraph?
- a. Optical illusions are very common in everyday life.
- b. Optical illusions make us think we see something that's not true.
- c. Optical illusions are the way we see things with our eyes.
- d. Optical illusions can only be seen by a few people.

Detail **2.** What causes optical illusion 1?
- a. All of the blue dots are the same color.
- b. We can see the blue dots clearly, but not the red dots.
- c. The red dots are not close to each other.
- d. We compare each red dot with the blue dots around it.

Detail **3.** What causes optical illusion 2?
- a. The white circles have small dark dots inside of them.
- b. The dark squares are much larger than the white circles.
- c. The difference between squares and circles confuses your brain.
- d. Your brain thinks that it can see white dots inside the dark squares.

Reference **4.** The word *They're* (line 13) refers to _____.
- a. dark dots
- c. dark squares
- b. white circles
- d. white dots

Paraphrase **5.** Another way to say *it keeps changing between the vase and the faces* (lines 19–20) is _____.
- a. First you see the vase, then the faces, then the vase again, and so on.
- b. Your mind decides to see the faces, but it can't see the vase anymore.
- c. The vase is the correct image, not the faces.
- d. The faces are really there, but the vase is not.

B. Summary. Complete the sentences below.
Fill in each blank with one word from the reading.

Introduction: *With optical illusions, you can be wrong about things you _____ with your eyes.*

Optical Illusion 1	Optical Illusion 2	Optical Illusion 3
The red dot on the left looks _____ than the red dot on the right. The dots are really the same _____.	*You might see dark dots inside the white circles, but the dots are not really _____.*	*The picture shows two things: a _____ and two _____. Your mind has to decide which thing it sees.*

Conclusion: *Sometimes your eyes see something, but your mind can't _____ it easily. That's called an optical illusion.*

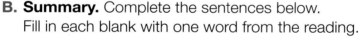

Vocabulary Practice

A. Completion. Complete the information using words from the box. Two words are extra.

> choose
> compared
> minds
> personal
> related
> size
> straightforward
> therefore

▲ Four sets of twins line up for a contest in Des Moines, Iowa, U.S.A.

Identical twins are born from the same egg. They are
1. _____ usually the same height and **2.** _____, and also have the same eye and hair color. Some researchers have found that the **3.** _____ of identical twins are similar too. For example, twins report that they often **4.** _____ to wear the same clothes on the same day, or say the same things at the same time. Identical twins may also have their own secret language, known only to each other. Because they are **5.** _____ in this special way, identical twins usually feel closer to each other **6.** _____ to other brothers and sisters.

B. Completion. Complete each sentence with the best answer.

1. If you make an error in a test, you write something _____.
  a. right   b. wrong

2. If something is personal, it's _____.
  a. for many people   b. only for you

3. If two things are related, they are _____.
  a. close   b. not close

4. If something is straightforward, it's _____ to understand.
  a. difficult   b. easy

5. If you have good vision, your _____ work well.
  a. ears   b. eyes

> ## Word Partnership
> Use **error** with:
> (v.) **make** an error, **correct** an error;
> (adj.) **common** error, **human** error.

7B

This class is interesting.

I'm angry!

I saw him last week.

The water is too hot.

A car is coming.

Sleep and Dreams

Before You Read

A. Labeling. Read the definitions below. Label the picture with the words in **blue**.

You have a **memory** when you think of something or someone from the past.

A **thought** is an idea that you have.

An **emotion** is a feeling such as happiness or sadness.

You feel a **sensation** when you touch something.

Visual **perception** helps you see and identify things.

B. Predict. Read the title and headings on the next page, and answer the questions below. Then read the passage to check your ideas.

1. How many dreams does the reading passage discuss?

2. What do you think the passage will tell you about those dreams?

THE MEANING OF DREAMS

1 Did you have any good dreams last night?

Dreams come from the part of the brain that contains memories, thoughts, and emotions. You dream during a stage of sleep called REM.[1] You can have up to six dreams a night, and each dream usually lasts from 10 to 40 minutes.

5 Whether or not people remember dreams depends on the individual. Some people remember many of their dreams while others do not.

But what do your dreams mean? Alan Siegel is a scientist who studies dreams. "Dreams help us get in touch with our deeper feelings," he says. "They can tell us a lot about ourselves, and may even help us figure out[2] problems."

10 Here are a few common dreams.

Dream 1: You Meet Someone When You Are Wearing Your Pajamas (or Nothing at All!)

This dream may be the result of an embarrassing[3] event in your life. Your brain is trying to help you deal with[4] the event.

15 **Dream 2: You're Flying**

This is a good period in your life. You may feel that other people look up to you as a leader.

Dream 3: You Didn't Study for a Test

This means you are under pressure. You are worried
20 about a major event in the future. If you're not prepared for the event, your dream could be telling you, "It's time to get to work!"

[1] **REM** (Rapid Eye Movement) is a stage of sleep when people dream.
[2] If you **figure out** a solution to a problem, you succeed in understanding it.
[3] If something is **embarrassing**, it makes you feel shy or ashamed.
[4] If you **deal with** a problem, you try to do something about it.

☐ Reading Comprehension

A. Multiple Choice. Choose the best answer for each question.

Main Idea **1.** What is the main idea of the reading?
- a. Everyone has dreams, but not everyone remembers them.
- b. Dreams come from only one part of the brain.
- c. Most people don't know what their dreams mean.
- d. Dreams can help us to understand ourselves and our feelings.

Detail **2.** Which of the following will you probably NOT have?
- a. a dream that lasts 15 minutes
- c. a dream that lasts 40 minutes
- b. a dream that lasts 25 minutes
- d. a dream that lasts 60 minutes

Paraphrase **3.** In line 8, another way to say *get in touch with* would be _____.
- a. talk to
- c. stay away from
- b. remember and then forget
- d. connect with and understand

Detail **4.** According to the passage, which of the following is true about dreams?
- a. If you dream you're wearing no clothes, something embarrassing probably happened to you.
- b. If you dream you are flying, this is probably a difficult time in your life.
- c. If you dream you didn't study for a test, you are probably not getting enough sleep at night.
- d. If you dream you didn't study for a test, then you have nothing to worry about.

Paraphrase **5.** In line 17, another way to say *look up to you* would be _____.
- a. are careful when they're with you
- c. like to talk to you
- b. think good things about you
- d. dream about you

B. Classification. Five people are describing an experience. Which dream from the passage will each person probably have? Write each answer (**a–e**) in the correct space (1–3).

- **a.** "I have to finish this paper tonight! If I don't hand it in on time, I'll get a bad grade!"
- **b.** "I felt terrible. I fell on the stairs, and everyone laughed at me!"
- **c.** "My life is great! I don't have any problems, and I'm really happy!"
- **d.** "Everyone else was wearing the right clothes. I just came in jeans and a T-shirt!"
- **e.** "The concert is in two days, and I haven't had much time to practice my violin!"

Vocabulary Practice

A. Completion. Complete the information using words from the box. Two words are extra.

contains	individuals	pressure
depend	major	stages
emotions	periods	
events	prepare	

We spend a(n) **1.** _____ part—about one-third—of our lives sleeping. During this time, our body grows stronger and our brain gets to rest. Humans need different amounts of sleep at different **2.** _____ of life. Children usually need more sleep compared to adults because they are still growing. Older people need to sleep for shorter **3.** _____ of time. Generally, most **4.** _____ need seven to eight hours of sleep a night.

A lot of people, however, don't get enough sleep. Many of us are under a lot of **5.** _____ because of the busy nature of modern life. This causes problems for the part of the brain that controls our **6.** _____.
For example, without enough sleep we become angry or worried easily.

If you have trouble sleeping, you should **7.** _____ for your sleep by taking a warm bath, listening to slow music, or drinking warm milk. Milk **8.** _____ melatonin, a chemical which causes us to feel sleepy.

▲ A child sleeps on the legs of its mother on the island of Sao Tome, off the west coast of Africa.

B. Definitions. Use the words in the box in **A** to complete the definitions.

1. _____ are important things that happen.

2. If something is _____, it is serious or important.

3. Another word for *people* is _____.

4. If you _____ for something, you make yourself ready for it.

5. When you _____ on something, you need help from it.

Usage

The noun **individual** is often used in formal or scientific English, and **person/people** in everyday speech:
> Twenty **individuals** took part in the experiment.
> There were twenty **people** at my birthday party.

Individual is also used as an adjective, e.g., *an **individual** decision.*

Parasomnia

A. Preview. Read the definition of *parasomnia*. Have you, or has anyone you know, experienced this problem? What other sleep problems might someone have?

Parasomnia par·a·som·ni·a (*n.*) a type of sleep disorder, or sleep problem, in which people move or act in an unnatural way while they are asleep, for example, talking or walking in their sleep

B. Summarize. Watch the video, *Parasomnia*. Then complete the summary below using words from the box. One word is extra.

| events | major | period | therefore |
| individuals | mind | stages | vision |

For people with *parasomnia*, getting a good night's sleep can be a
1. _____ problem. Parasomnia happens during the
2. _____ of time before REM sleep (the time when you dream). When you fall asleep, you go through four main
3. _____ before REM sleep. During this time, your heart and breathing relax, and your brain waves get slower. The thinking part of the brain—the **4.** _____ —is asleep. In some
5. _____, however, the part of the brain that controls the body is still awake. **6.** _____, these people are able to walk, talk, and do other things while they are still asleep. Most of these people cannot remember these **7.** _____ when they wake up the next day.

C. Think About It.

1. Do you get enough sleep? If you don't sleep well one night, do you feel different the next day?

2. What can people do to sleep better?

To learn more about the mind, visit elt.heinle.com/explorer

UNIT 8
Animal Wonders

Discuss these questions with a partner.

1. What's your favorite animal? Why?

2. What animals are special to people in your country?

3. Do you think animals have similar feelings to humans? Why do you think so?

▲ A male cat jumps in the snow in Germany.

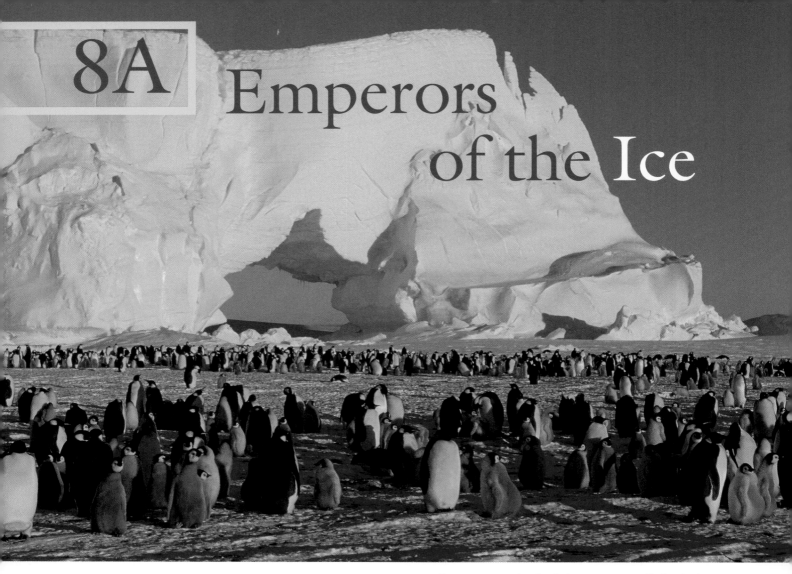

8A Emperors of the Ice

▲ Emperor penguins live in large groups called colonies.

☐ Before You Read

A. Quiz. What do you know about emperor penguins? Circle **True** or **False** for the sentences below. Then check your answers at the bottom of the page.

1. The emperor penguin is one of five kinds of penguins in Antarctica.	**True**	**False**
2. After the mother penguin lays an egg, she walks to the ocean.	**True**	**False**
3. As soon as the egg hatches,[1] the baby penguin walks to the ocean.	**True**	**False**
4. Emperor penguins learn to fly when they're about one year old.	**True**	**False**

[1] If a baby animal **hatches**, it comes out of an egg.

B. Predict. Look quickly at the photos, title, and headings on the next page. Check (✓) the information you think you'll read about. Then read the passage to check your answers.

❑ adult penguins and their babies

❑ young penguins getting older

❑ global warming and penguins

1) True. 2) True. 3) False. The baby walks to the ocean when it's about five months old. 4) False. Penguins can't fly.

A Penguin's Year

1 Saturday, May 23: **The Penguin Couple**

I've arrived at the colony[1]—a community of about 3,000 penguins. I'm studying two emperor penguins. I call the male "Scar"[2] (because of a mark on his back) and the female
5 "Sunrise." They walked over a hundred kilometers from the ocean to get here. Soon Sunrise will lay an egg. Then she'll walk back to the ocean to eat.

Tuesday, July 29: **Sharing the Work**

Penguin parents work together to raise a baby. For two
10 months, Scar has been keeping the egg warm. It's on top of his feet and under a special piece of skin called the "brood patch."

Sunrise returned yesterday, and the couple moved their egg from Scar's feet to hers. This is difficult for penguins. If the egg falls, it can freeze[3] quickly.

15 In this cold environment, Scar has lost almost half of his body weight. He needs to reach the ocean soon to catch and eat fish.

Wednesday, September 9: **New Life**

The baby has hatched! Scar returned yesterday. Now it's necessary for Sunrise to go to the ocean again.

20 Monday, October 19: **Growing Up**

The parents have made several trips[4] to the ocean for food. The baby is growing quickly.

Sunday, December 27: **Into the Water**

The baby is now on its own. Soon it will enter the water for
25 the first time. It will swim and eat until next April, and then return here. After a few more years, it too will start its own family.

[1] A **colony** is a group of people or animals of the same kind living together.
[2] A **scar** is a mark on the skin which is left after a cut has healed.
[3] If a liquid or something containing a liquid **freezes**, it becomes solid because of low temperatures.
[4] A **trip** is a journey that you make to a particular place.

Reading Comprehension

A. **Multiple Choice.** Choose the best answer for each question.

Gist
1. Another good title for this reading would be _____.
   a. A Study of a Penguin Family
   b. Penguins Around the World
   c. The Future of Wildlife in Antarctica
   d. The Life and Death of a Penguin

Detail
2. When does the male penguin care for the egg without the female?
   a. from May to July
   b. from July to September
   c. from September to October
   d. from October to December

Reference
3. The word *hers* (line 13) refers to _____.
   a. her movement   c. her feet
   b. her egg   d. her return

Inference
4. What will probably happen if the egg falls onto the ice?
   a. The parents will not be able to find the egg.
   b. The egg will break open and the baby will fall out.
   c. Another penguin will take the egg.
   d. The baby in the egg will die because of the cold.

Paraphrase
5. Another way to say *on its own* (line 24) would be _____.
   a. staying with its parents
   b. protecting its own egg
   c. living without its parents
   d. able to communicate

B. **Completion.** Complete the flow chart below. Fill in each blank with one or two words from the reading.

From Egg to Baby Penguin

1. A baby penguin's life begins when the mother penguin lays _____.

2. Penguin parents keep the egg warm on top of their _____ under a piece of _____.

3. It's difficult to do, but penguins must _____ their egg from one parent's feet to the other's, without letting it _____.

4. While one penguin parent keeps the egg warm, the other parent walks to _____ to eat.

5. When the egg hatches, the penguin parents see their _____ for the first time.

Vocabulary Practice

A. Matching. Read the information below and match each word in red with a definition.

- Siberian tigers grow to three meters (ten feet) in length and are the largest tigers in the world.

- They have thick fur because they live in a cold environment—the frozen forests of east Asia.

- Each tiger has a special pattern of black and orange marks on its fur. These make the tiger difficult to see when it is hunting.

- Tigers generally like to live alone. Male tigers leave their parents when they are still young.

- Most other types of cats do not like to enter water, but tigers love to swim.

1. father and mother   _____

2. natural conditions around a person or thing   _____

3. unusual; not like other kinds   _____

4. go into (something)   _____

B. Completion. Complete the information with words from the box. Two words are extra.

almost	communities	lay	necessary
catch	environment	special	raised

By the 1940s, the Siberian tiger had **1.** _____ disappeared. Hunting had left only 40 tigers living in the wild. Today, there are about 500 Siberian tigers in Asia, but only a few live in the wild. Most Siberian tigers today are **2.** _____ in zoos.

One problem is that in some Asian countries tiger body parts are used to make traditional medicines.[1] Some people therefore **3.** _____ and kill tigers to sell their body parts. Also, the Siberian tiger's forest home is under pressure from tree-cutting. As trees are cut down, the tiger's hunting ground gets smaller.

Many people believe it is **4.** _____ to create more laws to keep the tiger's natural **5.** _____ safe. Saving the tigers might also help the people who live around the area. When tourists come to see the tigers, they bring money and jobs to the local **6.** _____.

> ### Word Partnership
> Use **raise** with:
> raise **children**, raise **a family**, raise **horses/dogs**.
> Note: *raise (a family) = bring up (a family)*

[1] **Medicine** is any kind of drug used to treat a disease.

8B

Spider monkey, Bolivia

Animal Emotions

Chimpanzee, Tanzania

Lowland gorilla, West Africa

Labrador, Alaska

Orangutan, Washington D.C., U.S.A.

King penguins, South Georgia Island

☐ Before You Read

A. Discussion. Look at the photos. Which word(s) in the box would you use to describe each picture? Do you think animals really have these feelings?

anger	boredom	confusion	fear
happiness	love	surprise	

B. Scan. Quickly scan the passage on the next page. How many names can you find? Which are pets and which are humans? Read the passage to check your answers.

DO ANIMALS LAUGH?

1 We know animals can feel fear. They may also feel love since they have strong relationships with each other. So are animal emotions similar to our own?
5 And do animals have a sense of humor?

A PARROT NAMED BONGO

Sally Blanchard's parrot Bongo Marie didn't get along with her other parrot, Paco. In fact, it was obvious that Bongo
10 Marie didn't like Paco at all! One day, Blanchard cooked a chicken for dinner. She started to cut the chicken with a knife. "Oh! Paco!" said Bongo Marie loudly. Blanchard laughed
15 and said, "That's not Paco." "Oh . . . no," said Bongo Marie. This time, she sounded disappointed. Then the parrot laughed
20 at her own joke.[1]

YOGA DOG

Jean Donaldson enjoys doing yoga—and so does her dog Buffy. While Jean
25 sits in her yoga positions, Buffy carefully places her toys[2] on Donaldson's body. If a toy falls, Buffy runs to put it back on. Does this behavior have any real function? According to Donaldson,
30 "She thinks it's hilarious!"[3]

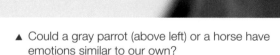

▲ Could a gray parrot (above left) or a horse have emotions similar to our own?

ANIMAL LAUGHTER

Can dogs "laugh"? Recent research shows that dogs tell each other when they want to play. In that situation, they make a special sound—a kind of "laugh." Psychologist Patricia Simonet recorded
35 the sound. Then she played it back to dogs to assess their response.[4] "All the dogs responded positively to the laugh," says Simonet.

So do animals have a sense of humor? If laughter is a clue,[5] then perhaps the answer is "yes!"

[1] A **joke** is something that makes you laugh.
[2] **Toys** are objects which people (usually children) or animals play with.
[3] If something is **hilarious**, it is very funny.
[4] Your **response** to something is your reply or reaction to it.
[5] A **clue** to a problem or puzzle is something that helps you find the answer.

☐ Reading Comprehension

A. Multiple Choice. Choose the best answer for each question.

Vocabulary

1. In line 8, the phrase *get along* is closest in meaning to _____.
   a. like to be   c. travel
   b. do things   d. stay close

Detail

2. Which of the following is NOT true?
   a. Paco and Bongo Marie are both parrots.
   b. Paco and Bongo Marie are good friends.
   c. Bongo Marie is Blanchard's parrot.
   d. Blanchard thinks Bongo Marie is funny.

Reference

3. The word *she* (line 19) refers to _____.
   a. the chicken   c. Paco
   b. Bongo Marie   d. Blanchard

Detail

4. Which of the following is true?
   a. Buffy laughs at Donaldson when she does yoga.
   b. Buffy feels sad when Donaldson does yoga.
   c. Donaldson thinks Buffy has a sense of humor.
   d. Buffy is worried that Donaldson doesn't like her.

Main Idea

5. What is the main idea of the last two paragraphs (from line 32)?
   a. A scientist showed that dogs talk to each other, so they seem to be funnier than most animals.
   b. A scientist showed that dogs make a laughing sound, so some animals might really have a sense of humor.
   c. A scientist recorded dogs making an unusual sound, but no one knows what it means.
   d. A scientist played with some dogs, and the dogs responded positively.

B. Completion. Complete each sentence in the chart with one or two words from the reading.

Do Animals Have a Sense of Humor?

Sally Blanchard: parrot owner	**1.** My parrot Bongo Marie told a _____ and laughed.
Jean Donaldson: dog owner	**2.** My dog likes to _____ on my body while I'm doing yoga.
Patricia Simonet: psychologist	**3.** Dogs make a sound that is similar to a _____.
	4. The sound lets other dogs know when they want _____.

Vocabulary Practice

A. Completion. Complete the information using the words from the box. Two words are extra.

assess	record
behavior	relationships
disappointed	sense
function	similar
obvious	situation

Monkeys are **1.** _____ to humans in many ways. For example, the **2.** _____ in a monkey family, such as between brother and sister, are often very close.

A team of researchers studied a pair of bonobo monkeys called Kanzi and Panbanisha. The brother and sister team had learned how to make knives from stone. So the researchers decided to **3.** _____ how good they were.

▲ Kanzi the bonobo is able to make knives from stone, play music, and understand more than 500 English words.

The researchers put a banana inside a box. Then they gave the bonobos what they needed to make a knife. The **4.** _____ of this knife was to cut open the box to get the banana. Kanzi made a very good knife, but his sister Panbanisha could not. Kanzi saw that his sister was feeling **5.** _____, and so he tried to give his knife to her. However, the scientists did not let him. Even in this **6.** _____, Kanzi knew what to do. When no one was looking, he put his knife where his sister could easily find it, and she finally got her banana. To the researchers, it was **7.** _____ from Kanzi's **8.** _____ that he really wanted to help his sister.

B. Definitions. Use the words in the box in **A** to complete the definitions.

1. If two things are _____, they are the same in some ways.

2. If something is _____, it is easy to see or understand.

3. A(n) _____ of something is a feeling or understanding of that thing.

4. If you _____ something, you test or measure it.

5. The _____ of a thing is what it is used for.

Word Partnership

Use **similar** with:
be + similar + **to**, e.g., *Animals **are similar** to humans in some ways.*

EXPLORE MORE

Penguins in Trouble

A. Preview. Read the information. What else do you know about penguins?

Emperor penguins are the largest of all penguins. An adult penguin stands about 115 cm (45 in), and weighs about 40 kg (88 lbs). Emperors live for about 15–20 years and stay together in groups called colonies. The male emperor penguin is the only animal that stays through the winter on Antarctica's open ice, where temperatures have been recorded as low as -60°C (-76°F)!

▲ A penguin faces a young Antarctic fur seal. Seals such as adult leopard seals often hunt penguins for food.

Antarctica

B. Summarize. Watch the video, *Penguins in Trouble*. Then complete the summary below with words from the box. Two words are extra.

assess	community	obvious	raise	similar
catch	loss	parents	sense	situation

In Antarctica, a(n) **1.** _____ of emperor penguins is going home after fishing. The penguin **2.** _____ need to look for food every day so that they can **3.** _____ their young. But a hungry leopard seal is also looking for food—penguins.

The seal decides to wait in the water and **4.** _____ its chances. Most of the penguins can **5.** _____ the danger, and they try to get away. The seal attacks and is able to **6.** _____ a penguin. But in this **7.** _____, the penguin does not fight back. Instead, it relaxes its body and waits for the seal to drop it. It gets away.

Later, another penguin is not so lucky. It's a(n) **8.** _____ for the penguin colony, as the seal swims away with its meal.

C. Think About It.

1. The video says, "For animals in Antarctica, every day is like the Olympic games." Why?

2. Which animals in your country do you think live in the most difficult environment?

To learn more about animals, visit elt.heinle.com/explorer

UNIT 9
Treasure
Hunters

Discuss these questions with a partner.

1. What's the most valuable thing you have ever found?

2. Do you know of any famous discoveries?

3. Why do you think people like looking for treasure?

▲ Workers look for gold at the Serra Pelada mine in Brazil.

97

9A Gold Fever

Empire[1] of the Inca

1438–1463
A royal son named Pachacuti, "Earth Shaker," becomes leader of the Inca tribes in 1438. Over time, the Inca under Pachacuti build roads and develop great cities like Cusco and Machu Picchu.

1463–1471
The Inca move north into land that is now part of Ecuador. They create many pieces of jewelry and other **objects** made of **gold**.

1471–1493
The Inca enlarge their empire until it measures nearly 4,000 km (2,500 miles) from north to south and includes as many as 16 million people.

1493–1527
After his father dies in 1527, a leader named Atahuallpa fights to become king. In 1532, Spanish **soldiers** under **commander** Francisco Pizarro arrive in Peru. Pizarro asks Atahuallpa to meet him in the town of Cajamarca. Atahuallpa thinks he is safe,[2] but he is walking into a trap[3]. . .

[1] An **empire** is a number of individual countries controlled by the government or ruler of one country.
[2] If a person or thing is **safe** from something, they cannot be harmed (hurt) by it.
[3] A **trap** is a trick designed to catch someone or something.

▲ The High Priest of the Sun, an Inca religious leader, holds up a golden bowl to the Inca gods.

▲ A gold statue of an Inca girl.

▲ Pizarro's sword can be seen today in the Gold Museum of Lima, Peru.

☐ Before You Read

A. Matching. Read the information above and match each word in **blue** with its definition.

1. _____ yellow metal that is very valuable
2. _____ items; things that have a certain shape or form
3. _____ a person in charge of a military unit, e.g., an army
4. _____ members of an army

B. Predict. Read the title and first paragraph on the next page. What do you think happened next? What was the "treasure"? Read the passage to check your ideas.

Lost Treasure of the INCA

▲ An illustration of Pizarro capturing the Inca Emperor Atahuallpa

1   The legend of the Inca gold begins in 1533, when the Inca were at war with the Spanish. The Spanish commander Francisco Pizarro captured[1] the Inca king Atahuallpa at his palace[2] in Cajamarca—now part of Peru.

    Pizarro made a deal with the Inca. He would let Atahuallpa go, but he demanded a
5 huge amount of gold. Pizarro received some gold, but then he told his soldiers to kill Atahuallpa. Angry at the murder[3] of their king, the Inca put the rest of the gold in a secret mountain cave.[4]

    Fifty years later, a poor Spanish soldier named Valverde fell in love with an Inca woman. The woman's family took him to see the treasure. He wrote an account of the trip and
10 explained how to find the gold.

    With Valverde's instructions, a Canadian named Barth Blake may have found the gold in 1886. In a letter, he wrote, "There are thousands of gold and silver pieces . . ." He also described ". . . the most incredible jewelry." Blake says he took a few of the objects. "I could not remove[5]
15 it alone," he said, "nor could thousands of men."

    No one knows whether Blake's story is true, as he disappeared[6] soon afterwards. Mark Honigsbaum, author of *Valverde's Gold*, thinks the gold was likely taken out centuries ago. "If not," he says, "and [if] it's still there, I think it's lost forever."

[1] If you **capture** someone or something, you catch them.
[2] A **palace** is a very large impressive house, usually the home of a king or queen.
[3] **Murder** is the crime of killing someone intentionally.

[4] A **cave** is a large hole in the side of a cliff or hill or under the ground.
[5] If you **remove** something from a place, you take it away.
[6] If someone or something **disappears**, they go or are taken away where nobody can find them.

☐ Reading Comprehension

A. Multiple Choice. Choose the best answer for each question.

Main Idea

1. What is the main idea of this reading?
   a. The story about the Inca gold came to us from Valverde.
   b. We may never know the truth about the Inca gold.
   c. Pizarro was the only person who ever saw the Inca gold.
   d. Barth Blake wrote a letter about finding the Inca gold.

Detail

2. The Inca king was named _____.
   a. Pizarro
   b. Atahuallpa
   c. Cajamarca
   d. Valverde

Reference

3. In line 5, *his* refers to _____.
   a. Pizarro's
   b. Atahuallpa's
   c. the Inca's
   d. Valverde's

Paraphrase

4. The *rest of the gold* (line 6) means the gold that _____.
   a. was still underground
   b. the Inca gave Pizarro
   c. Pizarro's soldiers had found
   d. the Inca had not given Pizarro

Main Idea

5. What is Mark Honigsbaum's opinion on the gold (lines 17–19)?
   a. People will probably find it in the future.
   b. People may have found it in the past.
   c. The story about the gold is almost certainly not true.
   d. Barth Blake probably took all of the gold.

B. True or False. According to the passage, are the sentences below true or false? Circle **T** (true), **F** (false), or **NG** (not given in the passage).

1. Pizarro wanted to live in the palace in Cajamarca.   T   F   NG

2. The Inca gave Pizarro some of the gold.   T   F   NG

3. Valverde was helped by an Inca family.   T   F   NG

4. Blake says he took away hundreds of valuable items.   T   F   NG

5. Honigsbaum wrote a book about the Inca gold.   T   F   NG

Vocabulary Practice

A. Matching. Read the information below. Then match each word in red with a definition.

The disappearance of the Amber Room is one of the greatest mysteries in the art world. The room was built using large amounts of precious stone called amber, which was then covered in gold and jewels. Visitors described the room as so beautiful that it could be the Eighth Wonder of the World.

In 1716, Tsar[1] Peter the Great received the room as a gift from the King of Prussia (now part of Germany) after the two countries made a peace deal. Over the years, the Russians made the room even bigger, using up to six tons (6,000 kilograms) of amber. In 1941, Germany took over parts of Russia. The Germans demanded that the Amber Room be given back to them. It was returned to Germany, where it was placed in a museum. By 1945, after the war had ended, the Russians found nothing left of the Amber Room. It had simply disappeared, never to be found again.

▲ This copy of the Amber Room in St. Petersburg, Russia, gives an idea of how beautiful the room was.

[1] **Tsar** was the name given to male rulers of Russia before 1917 (sometimes spelt *tzar* or *czar*).

1. to get something from someone who gives it to you _____
2. how much there is of something _____
3. an agreement with someone _____
4. to ask for something in a strong, forceful way _____
5. to say what something is like _____

B. Completion. Complete the information using words from the box. Two words are extra.

accounts	author	instructions	letters
amount	incredible	killed	receives

Near the end of World War II, Germany knew that it was losing. Its towns were being bombed, and many German soldiers had been **1.** _____. Fearing the Russians would take back the Amber Room, the government gave **2.** _____ to cut the room into pieces and hide them in boxes. However, the boxes went missing, and the Amber Room has not been found since.

What happened to the room? According to some **3.** _____, it was destroyed when the area was bombed. Some people believe that the boxes containing the treasure sank to the bottom of the ocean while being shipped. Others believe the room is hidden underground. If that is true, it would be a(n) **4.** _____ find for treasure hunters.

Larisa Bardovskaya is director of the Tsarskoye Selo museum, which housed the original Amber Room. Every year she **5.** _____ many **6.** _____ and emails about the Amber Room from people around the world. "We hear people saying they found the Amber Room three or four times a year," she says. Today visitors to the museum can see a copy of the room. That way, they can imagine what this incredible—and mysterious—room really looked like.

Usage

Number is used to describe how many there are of something: *The teacher was surprised at the large **number** of students in the class.* **Amount** is used to describe how much there is of something: *There is only a small **amount** of water in the glass.*

9B Precious Discoveries

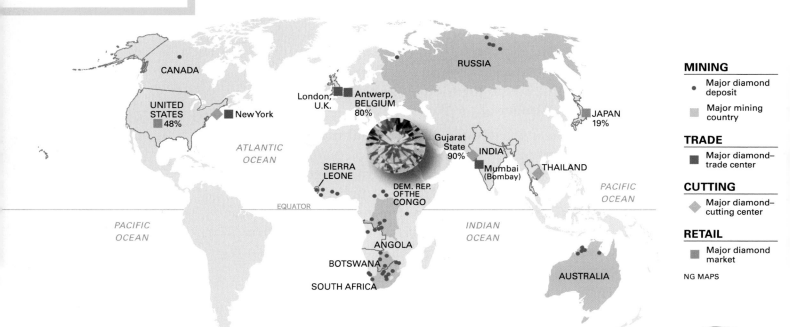

MINING
- Major diamond deposit
- Major mining country

TRADE
- Major diamond–trade center

CUTTING
- Major diamond–cutting center

RETAIL
- Major diamond market

NG MAPS

Diamond deposits[1] are found by mining[2] underground. The world's diamond mines produce about 800 million stones a year, but not all are good enough for jewelry. Eighty percent of jewelry diamonds pass through Antwerp, an important trading center. They are then cut and polished,[3] mostly in India. About half are then sold in the United States.

[1] A **deposit** is an amount of something that is left somewhere.
[2] When something is **mined**, it is taken from the ground by digging deep holes and tunnels (called **mines**).
[3] If you **polish** something, you make it shine, usually by rubbing it with a cloth.

Most diamonds ▶ are colorless, but some are orange, red, pink, blue, or other colors.

☐ Before You Read

A. Reading Maps. Look at the map and caption above and answer the following questions.

1. Which continent has the most diamond deposits? _____
2. In which country are most jewelry diamonds traded? _____
3. Other than India, where else are diamonds cut? _____
4. About one in five diamonds are sold in which country? _____

B. Scan. You are going to read about a famous diamond curse (something that causes bad luck). Quickly scan the reading to answer the questions below. Then read again to check your answers.

1. How many people are mentioned in the reading?
2. Which of these people have had bad luck?

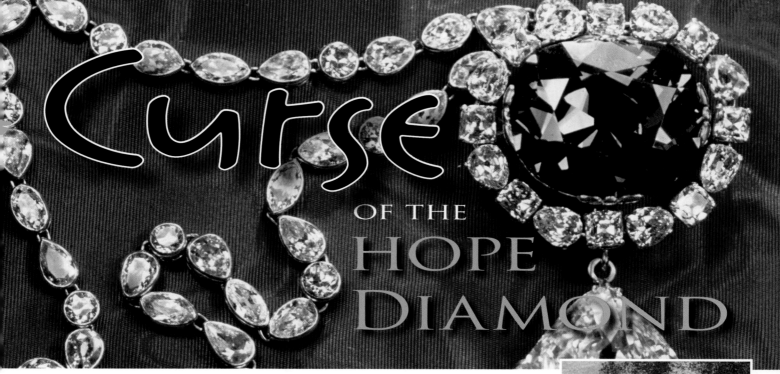

CURSE OF THE HOPE DIAMOND

The execution of King Louis XVI's wife, Marie Antoinette—a victim of the Hope Diamond (pictured above)?

1 　Diamonds have many special qualities. They're the hardest material on Earth. They sparkle[1] in the light. Some are incredibly expensive. But could a diamond bring 300 years of bad luck?

5 　✦ In 1668, the French royal family bought a large diamond from India. It became known as the "French Blue." When King Louis XVI and his wife were executed[2] in 1797, some people linked their deaths with the diamond's curse. (However, two earlier kings had worn the diamond 10　and not had bad luck.)

　✦ The Hope family bought the diamond in the 1830s. Soon after, Francis Hope's wife left him and he had to sell the diamond because of financial problems. The diamond then became known as the Hope Diamond.

15 　✦ Millionaire[3] Evalyn McLean loved jewelry—and stories of bad luck. In 1911, she had the opportunity to buy the Hope Diamond. Afterwards, two of her children died, and her husband became ill.

　✦ In 1958, a mailman[4] named James Todd brought the diamond to its present home at the Smithsonian Institution. Soon after, his wife died and his house burned down.

20 　So is there any truth to the supposed curse? Richard Kurin is the author of a book about the Hope Diamond. He rejects the idea of a curse. He believes the curse could be explained by chance. But other people don't accept that. For them, the Hope Diamond may just be waiting for its next victim[5] . . .

[1] If something **sparkles**, it is clear and bright and very shiny.
[2] To **execute** someone means to kill them as punishment.
[3] A **millionaire** is a person who is worth at least a million dollars.
[4] A **mailman** is someone who delivers letters and packages.
[5] A **victim** is someone who has been hurt or killed.

☐ Reading Comprehension

A. Multiple Choice. Choose the best answer for each question.

Gist

1. Another good title for the reading could be _____.
   a. The Hope Diamond and the French Royal Family
   b. The Hope Diamond: A Story of Bad Luck?
   c. The Hope Diamond's Next Victim
   d. History of the Hope Family

Sequence

2. Which of the following happened first?
   a. Francis Hope's wife left him.
   b. Evalyn McLean's husband became ill.
   c. James Todd took the diamond to the Smithsonian Institution.
   d. The Hope family bought the diamond.

Detail

3. For how long has the Hope Diamond been at the Smithsonian Institution?
   a. since 1797
   b. since 1830
   c. since 1911
   d. since 1958

Paraphrase

4. Another way to say *burned down* (line 19) would be _____.
   a. was lost in a storm
   b. was taken by the government
   c. was completely destroyed by fire
   d. was cursed by a diamond

Inference

5. Which statement would Richard Kurin probably agree with?
   a. All of the bad luck can be explained by chance.
   b. The curse probably made Evalyn McLean's husband ill.
   c. Several deaths have been caused by the curse.
   d. The Smithsonian Institution will probably have bad luck in the future.

B. Matching. Match each statement to the person who might have said it. One person is extra.

1. _____ "Maybe I'm lucky. The diamond was named for my family."

2. _____ "The diamond wasn't even mine! I just carried it for one day!"

3. _____ "I don't believe that bad things happen because of the diamond."

4. _____ "Why me? My family bought the diamond over 100 years ago!"

   a. King Louis XVI
   b. Francis Hope
   c. Evalyn McLean
   d. James Todd
   e. Richard Kurin

Vocabulary Practice

A. Completion. Complete the information using words from the box. One word is extra.

accepted	financial	presently
expensive	opportunity	supposed

People find treasures in some very unusual places. Dutch teacher Paul van den Heuvel was teaching his class about World War II, so he visited an antique[1] store to look for items from the 1940s. As he was looking at some old postcards, Paul was surprised to find one signed with the name "Anne Frank."[2] At first, van den Heuvel
1. _____ that the postcard wasn't real. Some experts examined the postcard carefully. They finally
2. _____ that the real Anne Frank had written it. The postcard became very **3.** _____ and is
4. _____ worth over $165,000. But perhaps it is really the postcard's historical, rather than
5. _____, value that is the most important.

[1] An **antique** is an item that has special value because of its age.
[2] **Anne Frank** (1929–1945) was a Dutch girl who wrote about her experiences in the war in a famous book that became known as *The Diary of a Young Girl*. She died in 1945, aged 15.

B. Matching. Read the information below. Then match each word in red with its definition.

One man found a treasure in his own house. Matt Rodgers was working on the electric wires of his house when he found a box inside the wall. It was full of coins—and a letter from a man to his family. The coins were made of silver and the material was of very good quality. Although Matt had the opportunity to keep the money for himself, he rejected that idea. The letter provided him with a link to the man's family, and finally he was able to find them. The family were very surprised at receiving the letter and very happy to accept the coins! Matt said: "It was the right thing to do."

1. how good or bad something is _____
2. to say yes or agree to take something _____
3. a chance _____
4. a connection between two things _____
5. to say no or disagree to something _____
6. a hard object, e.g., a metal _____
7. in the end; at last _____

▲ A statue in Amsterdam stands near the house where Anne Frank lived.

Usage

We use **indeed** mostly in formal English. Informally, we use **really**.
*The postcard was **indeed** from Anne Frank.* (formal)
*The letter was **really** from my friend.* (informal)

Lost Treasure of Afghanistan

A. Preview. Look at the photo and read the quotes. What do you think is happening?

" My heart was trembling. I was worried about the gold . . . I was worried about everything. "
— *Archeologist Fred Hiebert*

" It's like seeing an old friend again after 25 years. "
— *Archeologist Viktor Sarianidi*

▲ **April, 2004:** A group of people including Viktor Sarianidi (center, with white hair) and Fred Hiebert (center right, back) watch and wait as a box is opened in Kabul Museum, Afghanistan.

B. Summarize. Watch the video, *Lost Treasure of Afghanistan*. Then complete the summary below with words from the box. Two words are extra.

amount	incredible	opportunity
demanded	instructions	quality
described	kill	receive

In 1978, an archaeologist named Viktor Sarianidi discovered a(n) **1.** _____ treasure in Afghanistan—the Bactrian Hoard. He found more than 20,000 gold coins of very good **2.** _____. This was a very large **3.** _____ of gold, so it was put safely in the National Museum of Kabul. But when war came to Afghanistan, the Bactrian Hoard disappeared. Some people thought the army **4.** _____ the gold and took it out of the country. Others thought Sarianidi stole it. After the war ended, the new president of Afghanistan heard about a secret room in his palace with many boxes. Sarianidi and another archeologist Fred Hiebert had the **5.** _____ to go to Kabul for the opening of the boxes. The president gave **6.** _____ for the box to be cut open. Inside was the Bactrian Hoard. Sarianidi **7.** _____ it as one of the happiest moments of his life.

C. Think About It.

1. What might have happened to the people who had the keys to the box?

2. Viktor Sarianidi described finding the treasure as one of the luckiest and happiest moments of his life. Has there been a time in your life when you were very lucky?

To learn more about the treasure hunters, visit elt.heinle.com/explorer

A. Crossword. Use the definitions below to complete the missing words.

Across

7. easy to see or understand
8. Things that are ____ are like each other in some ways.
11. If something is ____, it is needed.
12. to go into
14. to disagree or say no to something
16. feelings like anger and sadness
18. as a result, in conclusion
19. mistake
20. costs a lot of money

Down

1. The ____ of a piece of writing is the person who wrote it.
2. a length of time
3. important, serious
4. how good or bad something is
5. to test how good something is
6. information on how to do something
9. to get ready for an event or action
10. to agree or say yes to something
13. If you ____ between two things, you decide which one you want.
15. to get something after someone gives or sends it to you
17. mother or father

B. Notes Completion. Scan the information on pages **108–109** to complete the notes.

Field Notes

Site: The Taj Mahal

Location: _____, India

Information:
- The Taj Mahal is one of the _____ of the World.
- It was built in the mid-17th century by Emperor _____ for his wife _____ to remember her after she died.
- It took over _____ years and _____ people to complete the Taj Mahal.
- The white stone has started to turn yellow because of bad _____.
- People are not allowed to drive cars near the monument. They must _____ or take the _____.
- According to legend, the emperor wanted to build a second Taj Mahal that was _____ in color.

A Love Poem in Stone

Site: **The Taj Mahal**

Location: **Agra, India**

Category: **Cultural**

Status: **World Heritage Site since 1978**

Agra, India

The Taj Mahal in Agra, India, is often called "a **poem** in stone." If so, it is really a love poem—and perhaps the most beautiful expression of love in the world.

The Taj Mahal was created by the **emperor** Shah Jahan in the mid-17th century for his favorite wife, Mumtaz Mahal. The royal couple lived happily together for 18 years, until Mumtaz died while giving birth to their 14th child. The emperor **promised** his wife before she died that he would build the most beautiful **monument** in the world to remember her.

More than 20,000 people, and a thousand elephants, worked for over 20 years to make the emperor's dream a reality. Soon after the Taj Mahal was finished, Shah Jahan's son took control of the country and became emperor. Shah Jahan was put in **prison**, where he lived until his death in 1666. The love story had a sad end, but the emperor's monument remains today, in the words of writer Salman Rushdie, "a lovely thing, perhaps the loveliest of things."

Taj Under Pressure

Up to four million people visit the Taj Mahal every year. As a result, air quality has become worse, and the white stone has started to turn yellow. To keep the environment clean, visitors are no longer able to drive cars near the monument, and instead have to walk or take an electric bus. It is hoped this will ensure a bright future for this incredible monument.

Glossary

emperor: the male ruler of an empire

monument: a large building to remind people of an event in history or a famous person

poem: an imaginative expression of ideas, experiences, and emotions, usually in the form of written or spoken words

prison: a building where people are kept for punishment

promise: say that you will do something

Truth or Legend?

There are many legends about the Taj Mahal. One legend says that after building was complete, Shah Jahan cut off the hands of the builders and put out the eyes of the designers. He supposedly didn't want them to make another building as beautiful as the Taj Mahal. Another legend says the emperor also planned to build a similar, black Taj Mahal on the other side of the river. Although interesting tales, most historians believe they are not true.

A 1630 painting shows ▶ Shah Jahan standing on a globe. In Persian, his name means "King of the World."

Wonder of the World

In 2007, the Taj Mahal was named as one of the Seven Wonders of the World by the New7Wonders Foundation. The list was the result of more than 100 million votes received online and by telephone from people around the world. The last remaining Wonder of the Ancient World—the Pyramids of Giza in Egypt—was included as a special "Eighth Wonder."

The New "Wonders of the World"

Chichen Itza	Yucatan, Mexico
The Colosseum	Rome, Italy
The Great Wall of China	China
Machu Picchu	Cusco, Peru
Petra	Jordan
Statue of Christ the Redeemer	Rio de Janeiro, Brazil
The Taj Mahal	Agra, India
The Giza Pyramids	Giza, Egypt

A. Dictionary Skills. In English, there may be different meanings for the same word. Read the definitions for each word in the box. Then write **1** or **2** next to the words in red below.

> **account** (*n.*) **1.** money deposited with a bank **2.** a written or spoken report of something that has happened
> **catch** (*v.*) **1.** to get or take something **2.** to get on a train, bus, or plane
> **raise** (*v.*) **1.** to move something so that it is in a higher position **2.** to take care of a baby until it is grown up
> **stage** (*n.*) **1.** one part of an activity or a process **2.** the area in a theater where actors act
> **vision** (*n.*) **1.** what you imagine or hope things will be like **2.** your ability to see with your eyes

1. Tigers usually hide in long grass before they try to catch _____ their prey.

2. The Inca leader's vision _____ was to have most of South America under his control.

3. Countries like Japan have low birth rates because it is expensive to raise _____ a child.

4. It takes a lot of training before an animal can appear in a movie or on stage _____.

5. Several Titanic passengers gave an account _____ of what happened on that night.

B. Word Link. The suffix **–able** changes a verb into an adjective. For example, if something is *acceptable*, you can accept it. Complete the sentences with the *–able* adjective of a verb in the box. Use your dictionary to help you.

accept	depend	enjoy	knowledge	value

1. Gold is _____ mainly because there is not much of it available.

2. Penguin parents are very _____ when it comes to finding food for their baby.

3. Scientist Alan Siegel is very _____ about dream psychology.

4. Richard Kurin thinks the Hope Diamond curse can be explained by chance, but some do not find that theory _____.

5. Theme parks and funhouses are popular because they are _____ for both children and adults.

WARM UP

Discuss these questions with a partner.

1. What do you think is the most important skill you learn in school?

2. What are schools like in your country? How are they different from schools in other countries?

3. If you could create your dream school, what would it be like?

10A
Learning in the Wild

Before You Read

A. Labeling. Read the information and label the animals pictured above (**1–4**).

Kruger National Park is one of the oldest and largest parks in Africa. It was first set up in 1898 to control[1] hunting and to protect the wildlife living there. Today it is home to an incredible variety of species, including more than 500 types of birds and about 150 different types of mammals. Among these are deer-like (**1**) **antelope** (like the steenbok and impala), (**2**) **elephants**, (**3**) **giraffes**, and a wild pig known as a (**4**) **warthog**.

[1] If you **control** an activity, you have power over how it is done.

B. Skim for the Main Idea. Look at the photos of Southern Cross School on the next page, and quickly skim the reading. What is unusual about this school? Read the passage again to check your ideas.

Nature's Classroom

1   Look around your classroom. Do you see students sitting at desks? Are teachers writing on a board and giving lectures? At Southern Cross School, near the famous Kruger National Park in South Africa, things are different. Here, nature is the classroom.

5   Both the park and the school are home to wild animals such as giraffes, impalas, and warthogs. Students at the school study the same subjects as other students in South Africa. But at Southern Cross, the staff and students go out into the wild to learn.

In one lesson, students apply the principles of mathematics to
10   the study of local wildlife. Younger students count how many kinds of animals drank at the nearby water troughs[1] during the night. Older students measure the amount of water the animals drank, and calculate[2] how much water the animals will need over weeks or months.

15   In language classes, a common topic is conservation. In one recent debate,[3] students discussed an important question: should people give water to wild animals during a drought?[4] Another project might consist of finding out how an animal died.

The director of the school is Ant de Boer. His aim is for students
20   to learn the importance of caring for the environment. De Boer says, "When they leave school, we want them to be champions of the natural environment." As the school motto[5] says, Southern Cross aims to be a "School for the Planet."

[1] A **trough** is a long, narrow container from which farm animals eat or drink.
[2] If you **calculate** a number or amount, you work it out using arithmetic.
[3] A **debate** is a discussion about a subject on which people have different views.
[4] A **drought** is a long period of time with no rain.
[5] A **motto** is a short sentence or phrase that describes the aims and beliefs of a group.

Reading Comprehension

A. Multiple Choice. Choose the best answer for each question.

Main Idea

1. Southern Cross is a special kind of school because
its students _____.
   a. don't study normal school subjects
   b. listen to a lot of lectures about nature
   c. use nature to study school subjects
   d. take care of animals in their classroom

Paraphrase

2. Which of the following is closest in meaning to *go out into the wild* (line 8)?
   a. go camping   c. go away
   b. go outdoors   d. go to school

Purpose

3. What is the purpose of the third paragraph (from line 9)?
   a. to give examples of how Southern Cross students study mathematics
   b. to describe the various subjects that students study at Southern Cross
   c. to explain how much water South African animals drink
   d. to show why it's important to learn about mathematics

Vocabulary

4. Which of these is a kind of *wildlife* (line 10)?
   a. students   c. animals
   b. mathematics   d. troughs

Detail

5. Which type of lesson goal is NOT mentioned?
   a. measuring how much water animals drink
   b. learning how an animal died
   c. talking about a conservation topic
   d. calculating how many animals there are in the park

B. Matching. Match the ending of each sentence (**a–e**) to its beginning.

1. _____ Southern Cross is close to

2. _____ Southern Cross is different from most schools

3. _____ To learn mathematics, students at Southern Cross

4. _____ To improve their language skills, students at Southern Cross

5. _____ The Southern Cross school wants students to

a. might have a debate about conservation.
b. take care of the environment after they leave.
c. Kruger National Park in South Africa.
d. might count how many animals drank at the troughs.
e. because students often have lessons in the wild.

Vocabulary Practice

A. Completion. Complete the information using words from the box. One word is extra.

aim	boards	lectures	principle	staff
apply	consists	local	project	topics

Utah in the United States is famous for its beautiful desert and national parks—and an unusual school called Boulder Outdoor Survival School (BOSS). The teaching **1.** _____ at BOSS follow an unusual **2.** _____: "know more, carry less." Their **3.** _____ is to teach people to survive in wild areas with no camping equipment. Teachers don't give **4.** _____ on math or science, nor do they teach students by writing on **5.** _____. Instead, BOSS brings students outside, where they learn about **6.** _____ like making fires, finding water in the desert, and learning about **7.** _____ plants. Students then **8.** _____ the lessons they have learned during 30-mile (48-km) hikes. A student's final exam **9.** _____ of going into the desert alone for three days with only a few simple tools. Even though it's difficult, students say it's an incredible and valuable experience.

▲ Many movies have been filmed in Utah's famous rocky desert.

B. Definitions. Use the words in the box in **A** to complete the definitions.

1. If you _____ something, you use it in an activity.
2. A(n) _____ is a belief about the way you should act.
3. A(n) _____ is a study or piece of research.
4. The _____ of something is your purpose for doing it.
5. The _____ of an organization is all the people who work for it.

Usage

Staff is a singular noun for a group of people: *The **staff** was very happy about the holiday party.*
Use **a member of the staff** to talk about one person: ***A member of the staff** thanked the boss for the party.*

10B

THE DIGITAL DECADE

2000 About 20 million websites are online.

2001 About 500 million people use the Internet.

2004 **Social networking** site Facebook is launched.[1]

2005 **Video sharing** site YouTube is launched.

2007 Number of Internet users: over 1 billion. Number of **blogs**: 100 million.

2008 Number of individual web pages: about 1 trillion (1,000,000,000,000). Number of searches using Google **search engine**: about 2 billion every day.

2009 50% of web users in China (about 150 million people) use **mobile**[2] **Internet**.

[1] If something is **launched**, it is started.
[2] If something is **mobile**, it can be moved from place to place easily (e.g. a *mobile phone*).

Classroom of the Future

WHAT DOES IT MEAN TO BE A STUDENT TODAY? That's one question Michael Wesch is always asking. Wesch is a professor at Kansas State University, U.S.A. In 2008, he was named U.S. Professor of the Year. He explores how the Internet and new media are changing the way we learn. "Technology is connecting us in ways never seen before in human history," he says. In 2007, he created a video called "Web 2.0 . . . The Machine is Us/ing Us." The video quickly got over 10 million views on YouTube.

☐ Before You Read

A. Discussion. Look at the timeline and information above. Discuss the questions with a partner.

1. Which of the services above in **blue** have you used before? How often do you use them?

2. How do you use the web for learning? Is the way you learn different from how you learned five years ago?

B. Predict. Read the interview questions on the next page. How do you think Michael Wesch will answer them? Read the interview to check your ideas.

AN INTERVIEW WITH MICHAEL WESCH

1   HOW HAS TECHNOLOGY CHANGED THE WAY WE LEARN?

Most importantly, the web now gives us the opportunity to publish our own work.
Instead of simply watching TV, we can create and edit our own videos. Instead of
just reading a magazine, we can write our own articles and documents and publish
them. There are now 1.4 billion people connected online, so we can use the work
we create to reach out and connect with large numbers of people.

WHAT ADVICE WOULD YOU GIVE TO TODAY'S STUDENTS AND TEACHERS?

Now is the time to rethink the meaning of the word "literacy." We used to think of
literacy as the ability to read and write. Now we need to think beyond reading and
writing. We all need to learn how to create and collaborate[1] on videos, photos, blogs,
wikis, online forums,[2] and other kinds of digital media.

This can be difficult when teachers and students do not have access[3] to the Internet,
but the core skills can be practiced in classrooms without technology. One of the
most important skills we must now learn is collaboration, and this can be practiced
on a chalkboard, whiteboard, or even a simple piece of paper. We can learn to listen
to one another, use each other's strengths, and practice working together in
any environment.

[1] When people **collaborate**, they work together on a particular project.
[2] A **forum** is a place or group in which people exchange ideas and discuss issues.
[3] If you have **access** to something, you are able to see it or use it.

☐ Reading Comprehension

A. Multiple Choice. Choose the best answer for each question.

Main Idea
1. What is the main idea of the first paragraph (from line 2)?
 a. Most people now watch a lot of movies and TV on the Internet.
 b. People used to read a lot of articles in the past, but not anymore.
 c. People now spend too much time connecting with other people using the Internet.
 d. The Internet allows us to create our own work and connect with many people.

Reference
2. The word *them* (line 5) refers to _____.
 a. TV and video
 b. articles and documents
 c. 1.4 billion people
 d. students and teachers

Main Idea
3. What is Michael Wesch's main idea in the second paragraph (from line 8)?
 a. Most teachers today do not teach literacy.
 b. Today's students no longer need to learn how to read and write.
 c. Today's students need to learn more than just reading and writing.
 d. Schools should teach digital literacy and not reading and writing.

Detail
4. What kind of digital media is NOT mentioned in the passage?
 a. blogs   c. e-mail messages
 b. photos   d. online forums

Inference
5. What would Michael Wesch probably say to a teacher without Internet access?
 a. "Teach your students how to collaborate in other ways."
 b. "Teach your students how to use other kinds of technology."
 c. "Teach your students how to write on a whiteboard."
 d. "Teach your students how to get access to the Internet."

B. Completion. Complete the diagram below. Fill in each blank with one word or number from the reading.

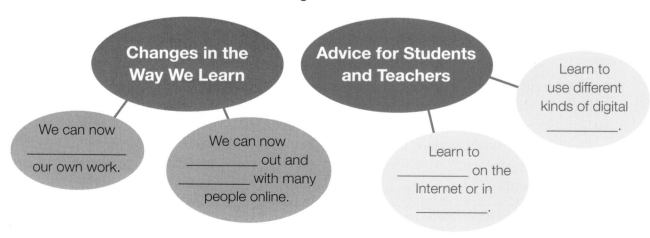

Changes in the Way We Learn

We can now _____ our own work.

We can now _____ out and _____ with many people online.

Advice for Students and Teachers

Learn to _____ on the Internet or in _____.

Learn to use different kinds of digital _____.

Vocabulary Practice

A. Completion. Complete the information using words from the box. One word is extra.

ability	digital
documents	edit
connect	practice
create	skills

▲ Children in Sierra Leone learn how to use OLPC computers.

Computer **1.** _____ are becoming increasingly important for students around the world. But this new kind of **2.** _____ education has not yet reached children in poor countries. A group called One Laptop Per Child (OLPC) is trying to change this. It was able to **3.** _____ a very small, simple laptop computer that costs only US$100. It gives these computers to schools in poor countries. This gives young children the **4.** _____ to use computers and go on the Internet. Computers help them learn about the world around them. It also lets them **5.** _____ their English or other foreign languages. Instead of using pen and paper, they can **6.** _____ their work easily on the computer and with other students. The aim of OLPC is to **7.** _____ children in every country around the world.

B. Words in Context. Complete each sentence with the best answer.

1. You can see articles in a _____.
   a. magazine   b. movie

2. If you connect two things, you _____.
   a. move them away from each other   b. put them together

3. The core of something is the _____ part.
   a. expensive   b. important

4. If you edit some writing, you _____ it.
   a. read   b. change

5. A skill is something that you _____.
   a. buy   b. learn

> **Word Partnership**
>
> Use **document** with:
> **create a** document, **edit a** document,
> **save a** document, **delete a** document.

Maasai Teacher

A. Preview. Read the quote below. What do you think Joseph Lekuton means by "we all have our own lions"?

▲ Maasai children spend much of their life taking care of cattle and other animals.

" The symbol of bravery in my community is the lion. Having faced that lion when I was 14 . . . changed everything for me. So . . . I think we all face challenges in life and we all have our own lions. "

– Joseph Lekuton, teacher and
Maasai tribesman

B. Summarize. Watch the video, *Maasai Warrior*. Then complete the summary below with words from the box. Two words are extra.

ability	apply	core	lectures	project
aim	consists	document	principles	skills

Joseph Lekuton is a teacher in Northern Virginia. He gives **1.** _____ to his students about American history. But his own country, Kenya, is very different. Joseph is a Maasai tribesman. Maasai children lead a very different life from American children. A ten-year-old's day **2.** _____ of taking care of cattle all day long. Maasai children also learn **3.** _____ like how to survive in the wild. Unlike many Maasai children, Lekuton was very lucky and went to school. With his **4.** _____ to speak English, he was able to study and teach in America. Lekuton wrote a book about his childhood called *Facing the Lion*. His **5.** _____ is to help children learn about a culture that's very different from their own. He also wants to teach them **6.** _____ like strength and hope, which they can **7.** _____ in their own lives. Joseph hopes that his first **8.** _____ will help children face their own lions.

C. Think About It.

1. Would you rather lead the life of a Maasai child or an American child? Why?

2. What "lions" do you face in your life?

To learn more about the future of education, visit elt.heinle.com/explorer

UNIT11
Giants of the Past

Discuss these questions with a partner.

1. What is the biggest animal in your country?

2. Do you know of any animals that are extinct (no longer living)?

3. If you could bring back an extinct animal, what would you bring back?

▲ A *Deinosuchus*, an extinct type of alligator, jumps out of the water at an *Albertosaurus*.

121

Mammoth!

11A

▲ The body of a baby mammoth is carried outside to be refrozen after being examined by scientists in Salekhard, Russia.

Salekhard, Russia

☐ Before You Read

A. Matching. Read the information below. Match each word in **blue** with its definition.

Tens of thousands of years ago, elephant-like creatures called *woolly mammoths* walked the Earth. They were related to modern elephants, but were different in some ways:

	Woolly mammoth	Modern elephant
Appearance	Long thick hair Long curved **tusk**	Thick skin but very little hair Short and straight tusk
Environment	Lived during the **Ice Age** in North America and Siberia	Lives in hot environments like India and Africa
Status	Became **extinct** 8,000–12,000 years ago	Total population today: 470,000–690,000 African elephants, and about 60,000 Asian elephants (pictured left)

1. _____ a long, pointed tooth used to fight or to find food

2. _____ a period when much of the earth was covered in ice

3. _____ no longer existing or living; completely died out

B. Predict. Look at the photo, illustrations, and captions on the next page. What do you think happened after this mammoth died? Read the passage to check your ideas.

The Mammoth's Tale

1 **Imagine finding a body that had been lost for 40,000 years...**

The strange animal in the ice looked like it was sleeping. Ten-year old Kostia Khudi and his brother had never seen anything like it before. But they had heard stories of the *mamont*, an imaginary animal that
5 lived in the frozen blackness of the Siberian underworld.[1] Their father, a reindeer herder[2] named Yuri Khudi, went to ask a friend for advice.[3] But when he returned, the body had disappeared . . .

Yuri soon found the animal's body leaning[4] against a store in a nearby town. (While he was away, his cousin had sold it to the store owner
10 for two snowmobiles.[5]) Dogs had eaten part of the tail and ear, but overall, it was still in "as close to perfect condition as you can imagine," says scientist Daniel Fisher. With help from the police, the body was taken by helicopter to a museum. The animal was a baby mammoth, and scientists called it Lyuba, after Yuri's wife.

15 From Siberia, the mammoth was sent to the Netherlands and Japan for analysis. Detailed studies of her teeth showed she was just one month old when she died. Ongoing research has also showed us the sequence of events that led to her death. Lyuba fell to her death near a muddy river. The mud helped
20 keep her body frozen until she was found 40,000 years later. Scientists hope that further analysis will help explain how mammoths such as Lyuba lived— and why they finally all died out.

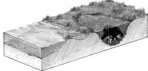

▲ Lyuba died when she fell into wet mud near a river.

▲ As the ground froze, her body shrank (became smaller).

▲ In 2006, melting caused Lyuba's body to wash free.

[1] The **underworld** is below the surface of the earth.
[2] A **herder** looks after a large group of animals of one kind.
[3] If you give someone **advice**, you tell them what you think they should do in a particular situation.
[4] If you **lean** on or against something, you rest against them.
[5] A **snowmobile** is a small vehicle for driving in snow.

Reading Comprehension

A. Multiple Choice. Choose the best answer for each question.

Gist

1. The article is mainly about _____.
   a. Yuri Khudi's life in Siberia
   b. animals that are now extinct
   c. an important discovery
   d. what life was like for Lyuba

Detail

2. What happened first?
   a. Yuri's cousin sold the mammoth to a store owner.
   b. Yuri went to ask a friend for advice.
   c. Lyuba's body was taken to a museum.
   d. The police arrived to take Lyuba's body away.

Purpose

3. What is the purpose of the second paragraph?
   a. to describe the condition of Lyuba when she was found
   b. to describe the difficulties of analyzing a mammoth body
   c. to explain how Lyuba was found again and taken to a safe place
   d. to explain how scientist Daniel Fisher came to Siberia to study Lyuba

Reference

4. The word *it* (line 11) refers to a(n) _____.
   a. body
   b. store
   c. tail
   d. ear

Paraphrase

5. Which of the following is closest in meaning to *all died out* (line 23)?
   a. became extinct
   b. killed each other
   c. moved to another place
   d. died at a young age

B. True or False. According to the passage, are the sentences below true or false? Circle **T** (true), **F** (false), or **NG** (not given in the passage).

1. Yuri Khudi's job is to take care of a group of animals.	**T**	**F**	**NG**
2. Yuri Khudi has more than two sons.	**T**	**F**	**NG**
3. Yuri Khudi's wife is also named Lyuba.	**T**	**F**	**NG**
4. Lyuba's body has been in at least three countries.	**T**	**F**	**NG**
5. Lyuba's teeth showed that she was a year old when she died.	**T**	**F**	**NG**

Vocabulary Practice

A. Completion. Complete the information using words from the box. Two words are extra.

analysis	imagine	ongoing	perfect
details	nearby	overall	sent

1. _____ a crocodile with more than 100 teeth and so big that it eats dinosaurs! Scientists say such a crocodile really did live 110 million years ago in Africa. It was so huge that they called it "SuperCroc."

For a long time not much was known about SuperCroc, as scientists only had a few bones and teeth. But, in 2000, Paul Sereno and his team found an area in the Sahara Desert that was full of SuperCroc bones. **2.** _____, they had enough bones to put together about 50 percent of SuperCroc's body.

▲ Members of Paul Sereno's team uncover the remains of an ancient crocodile in the Sahara desert.

From their work, the team learned many **3.** _____ about SuperCroc's life. For example, they now know that it grew to the size of a bus and weighed about 8,000 kilograms (17,500 pounds). Its strong jaws and big teeth were
4. _____ for catching and holding prey. After his examination, Serano
5. _____ SuperCroc's bones to the U.S. for further **6.** _____.
The bones are now on display in museums to teach people about this amazing animal.

B. Words in Context. Complete each sentence with the best answer.

1. If something is ongoing, it is _____.
   a. finished   b. not finished

2. If something leads to another, it goes _____ it.
   a. toward   b. away from

3. If something is nearby, it is _____.
   a. close   b. far

4. If something is in sequence, it happens _____.
   a. one after another   b. at the same time

5. If you send something, you _____ it.
   a. get   b. give

Usage

Analyses is the plural form of **analysis**: *Scientists did an* **analysis** *of the animal's bones. They also did* **analyses** *of the animal's skin and hair.*

11B Monsters of the Deep

Before You Read

A. Labeling. Read the information below. Then label the picture with the words in **blue**.

At 14 meters (45 feet) long, *Tylosaurus* was one of the biggest sea monsters of all time. By looking at fossils, scientists know that *Tylosaurus* was a strong **predator** with great **jaws** and sharp **teeth**. Analysis of its **stomach** contents shows that its **prey** included fish, seabirds, and even sharks. It used its long **tail** to push itself through the water and its two shorter **fins** to change direction. Although *Tylosaurus* was not related to the dinosaurs, it lived and became extinct around the same time.

B. Predict. Look quickly at the title, headings, pictures, and captions on the next page and answer the questions below. Then read the passage to check your answers.

1. How many sea monsters does the passage mention?

2. What do you think was unusual about each animal?

When GIANTS Ruled the Sea

1   Sea monsters are not just imaginary creatures.[1] Real ones did indeed live on Earth millions of years ago. Fossils[2] have helped scientists make very real-looking models of these huge creatures. The fossils also help us understand some of the animals' unusual characteristics.

▲ *Temnodontosaurus*

Eyes in the Dark

5   *Temnodontosaurus* was certainly an unusual animal. It had some of the largest eyes in nature—more than 25 cm (10 inches) across! With a name that means "cutting tooth lizard," *Temnodontosaurus* could easily pick out its prey in the dark water.

Terror of the Deep

10   *Kronosaurus* lived in the seas that covered Australia, but it probably left the water to lay its eggs on land. Its head was seven feet (2 m) long and its teeth were as big as bananas! The prime function of a set of teeth like this, says paleontologist Colin McHenry, was
15   to grab and crush its prey. In fact, *Kronosaurus* was one of the most powerful predators of all time.

▲ *Kronosaurus*

The Stalker[3]

Thalassomedon was a sea monster with a very long neck. It also had a special means of catching fish: it carried stones
20   in its stomach! These helped keep the largest portion of its body down in the dark water while the long neck slowly rose up toward the fish. The fish had no defense against *Thalassomedon*—they didn't see the huge animal until it was too late!

▲ *Thalassomedon*

[1] A **creature** is any living thing that is not a plant.
[2] **Fossils** are the hard remains of animals or plants that lived millions of years ago.
[3] To **stalk** someone or something is to follow slowly and quietly.

☐ Reading Comprehension

A. Multiple Choice. Choose the best answer for each question.

Main Idea
1. What is the main purpose of the passage?
   a. to describe the three most dangerous sea predators of all time
   b. to describe three ancient sea animals with unusual characteristics
   c. to explain how and when the fossils of three sea animals were discovered
   d. to explain the main stages for creating a model of an ancient sea creature

Reference
2. The word *ones* (line 1) refers to _____.
   a. sea monsters   c. millions of years
   b. imaginary creatures   d. fossils

Detail
3. Which statement about *Kronosaurus* is NOT true?
   a. It lived in the sea that used to cover Australia.
   b. It stayed in the water all the time.
   c. Its teeth were very large.
   d. It was a very dangerous predator.

Vocabulary
4. In line 19, the word *means* could be replaced by _____.
   a. hunger   c. hope
   b. image   d. way

Inference
5. Why were fish probably not very afraid of *Thalassomedon*?
   a. The fish didn't see *Thalassomedon* as it came near.
   b. The fish were friendly with *Thalassomedon*.
   c. The fish were also predators, not just prey.
   d. The fish did not have very long necks.

B. Classification. Complete the notes using information from the reading. Write one word in each space.

	Temnodontosaurus	*Kronosaurus*	*Thalassomedon*
Unusual characteristics	had very large _____	teeth were the size of _____	had a very long _____, and had _____ inside its stomach
Special abilities	could easily see its _____ in the dark	could grab and _____ other animals	was able to reach _____ without being seen

Vocabulary Practice

A. Completion. Complete the information using words from the box. Two words are extra.

characteristics	models
crush	portions
defense	prime
indeed	probably
grab	set

▲ In 2006, researcher Tsunemi Kubodera took this photo of a giant squid caught near a Japanese island. A normal size squid is in the bottom right of the photo.

For hundreds of years, people have reported monsters attacking ships out in the ocean. Now we know that these "monsters" were
1. _____ giant squid.

Giant squid share many of the same
2. _____ as other types
of squid, like having eight arms and two longer tentacles. But giant squid are much, much bigger—females can grow up to 13 meters (43 feet) and males grow up to 10 meters (33 feet). They also have the biggest eyes of any animal in the world. Giant squid normally eat deep-sea fish and other types of squid. They use their large **3.** _____ of arms to quickly
4. _____ their prey as it swims by. Their only natural enemies are certain kinds of whales. As a **5.** _____ against such attackers, squid shoot ink into the water before they swim away.

For many years, scientists were unable to catch a giant squid on film. Instead, they found
6. _____ of its body in the stomachs of whales that eat squid. The scientists were able to use these body parts to make **7.** _____ of what the squid might look like. The first photos of a live giant squid were taken in 2004, and it is **8.** _____ as monstrous as people believed!

B. Definitions. Use the words in the box in **A** to complete the definitions.

1. If you _____ something, you press it very hard so that it breaks.

2. _____ are features that are usual for someone or something.

3. _____ are representations that show how something looks.

4. Something that is _____ is the most important.

5. A _____ is something you use or do to protect yourself from attack.

> ### Usage
>
> **Means** is a singular noun, so we use it with "a" or with numbers.
> *For squid, changing colors is a **means** of defense.*
> *Cats have two **means** of defense: their teeth and their claws.*

Dinosaurs

A. Preview. Look at the picture and read the caption. Can you see any similarities between the three animals?

B. Summarize. Watch the video, *Dinosaur*. Then complete the summary below with words from the box. Two words are extra.

characteristics	led
crush	nearby
defense	ongoing
details	prime
indeed	sequence

▲ Birds and dinosaurs may be linked by a common relative called *Archaeopteryx* (the middle picture), one of the earliest known birds.

Dinosaurs lived on Earth for about 150 million years, far longer than humans have been around. Some were very large, such as a long-necked sauropod called *Jobaria*. It weighed 25 tons (50,000 pounds) and ate a large amount of plants every day. *Jobaria* lived together in groups for **1.** _____ against meat-eating dinosaurs.

No one really knows about the **2.** _____ of events that **3.** _____ to all dinosaurs dying out 65 million years ago. Some scientists believe the **4.** _____ reason is that a rock from space hit the earth and created a lot of dust in the air. The dust stopped the sun's heat and light from reaching the earth, and dinosaurs died from the cold.

But, in a way, perhaps dinosaurs are still with us today. Many scientists believe that birds are related to dinosaurs. Birds have a lot of the same **5.** _____ as dinosaurs—for example, they lay eggs and keep them warm by sitting on them. Their bones are also very similar. **6.** _____ research is being carried out to discover more **7.** _____ about how these two kinds of animals are connected. In this way, scientists hope to find out whether birds are **8.** _____ living dinosaurs.

C. Think About It.

1. What are some other ways that birds and dinosaurs are similar?

2. Why do you think people like to watch movies and read stories about monsters?

To learn more about giants of the past, visit elt.heinle.com/explorer

UNIT12
Technology

Discuss these questions with a partner.

1. What kinds of technology do you often use?

2. How will life 30 years from now be different from today?

3. What do you think life will be like 100 years from now?

12A Robot Revolution

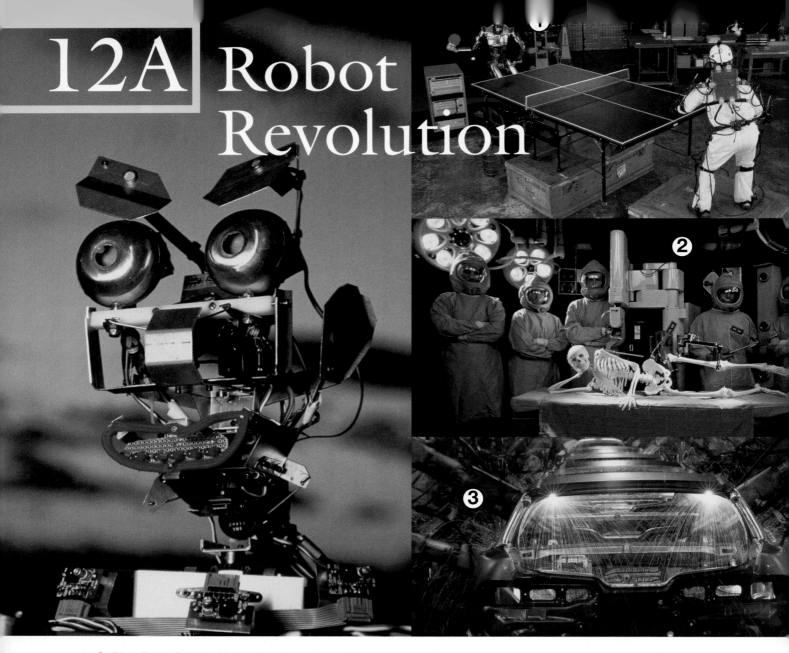

① **Ping Pong Robot** – At a research center in Utah, scientists train robots to play table tennis using human-like movements.
② **Robo Docs** – At Pittsburgh Shadyside Hospital, doctors show how they use a robot called ROBODOC to help in operations.
③ **Driving Forces** – For more than 30 years robots have worked on car production lines in Japan.

Before You Read

A. Discussion. What things can robots do that humans can't? What can humans do that robots can't? Use the words from the box or your own ideas.

run	climb stairs	play soccer	show emotions	feel emotions
jump	write poems	work in space	walk on water	walk upside down

B. Scan. Look quickly at the reading. Which of the things above are mentioned in the reading? Do you think today's robots can do them? Read the passage to check your ideas.

THE ROBOTS ARE COMING!

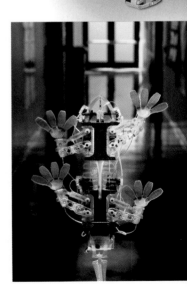

1　It's 2035. You're at a soccer game when suddenly . . . it's a goal! A robot player has scored!

A robot? Is this possible? Maybe. Scientists are working to create robots that can play sports like soccer. A robot with these skills
5　might also be able to aid humans—for example, by doing dangerous or difficult jobs, like putting out fires or catching criminals.[1]

Robots have changed greatly since they were first developed for use in industry. Whereas earlier machines were unable to operate by themselves, a modern robot like Asimo can walk by itself, climb
10　stairs, and even run slowly.

Then there is Kismet. It has eyes, lips, and ears that move in different ways to show surprise, happiness, anger, and other emotions. Robots like Kismet could show us how they "feel" about learning new things.

ANIMAL-BOTS

15　Scientists are also working on robots that look and act like animals. NASA has researched using robot snakes as an alternative to vehicles[2] with wheels. Snake-bots can't run or jump, but they can enter holes and move over rough ground. They might one day help scientists look for signs of life on Mars.

20　Other robots are designed to do a single task. The frog-bot can jump over objects. The sticky-bot can walk upside-down on the ceiling.[3] There's even a robot called Water Runner that can walk on water.

But will a robot soccer team exist by 2035? They
25　may even be world champions!

[1] A **criminal** is a person who has committed a crime.
[2] A **vehicle** is a machine that carries people or things around, like a car.
[3] The **ceiling** of a room is its top inside surface.

▲ In 2035, robots like Asimo (top) and the sticky-bot (above) may be part of our everyday lives.

Reading Comprehension

A. Multiple Choice. Choose the best answer for each question.

Gist
1. The article is mainly about _____.
   a. things robots can do
   b. why people need robots
   c. how to make your own robot
   d. robots of the future

Purpose
2. What is the main purpose of the third paragraph (from line 7)?
   a. to describe how the earliest robots were used in industry
   b. to explain why today's robots are different from early robots
   c. to explain why early robots could not do things by themselves
   d. to describe how the robot Asimo is able to walk by itself

Detail
3. Which robot is most able to show its feelings?
   a. Asimo   c. Snake-bot
   b. Kismet   d. Water Runner

Reference
4. The word *they* (line 17) refers to _____.
   a. vehicles   c. snake-bots
   b. wheels   d. holes

Inference
5. Which statement would the author probably agree with?
   a. It is not fair that robots have to do difficult jobs for humans.
   b. The robot Kismet can really feel human emotions.
   c. A frog-bot can do more tasks than a sticky-bot.
   d. Robot soccer players really could exist by 2035.

B. Completion. According to the article, does each sentence describe human-like robots, animal-bots, or both? Write each answer (**a–e**) in the correct place on the diagram.

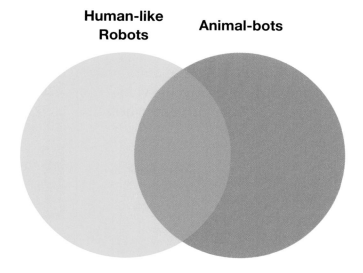

Human-like Robots   **Animal-bots**

a. It can run slowly.
b. It can walk upside down.
c. It can show emotions.
d. It might one day be able to help humans.
e. It can walk on water.

Vocabulary Practice

A. Completion. Complete the information using words from the box. One word is extra.

aid	operate
alternative	rough
dangerous	signs
exist	single
industries	whereas

Scientists in South Korea have developed a new robot called EveR-1 that can do many amazing things. Most robots that **1.** _____ today are used in heavy **2.** _____ like car-making. They **3.** _____ machines and do jobs that are boring or too **4.** _____ for people. In contrast, EveR-1 is a new kind of robot called a *service robot*. It does not look like your average robot—its face can show **5.** _____ of emotions like happiness and sadness, and it can even talk to people. Most robots look like machines, **6.** _____

▲ South Korea's human-like robot EveR-1 was followed in 2006 by EveR2-Muse (pictured above at Robot World in Seoul). According to its creator, KITECH, EveR2 is designed to represent a Korean woman in her 20s. EveR2 can show emotions like happiness and anger and can also sing. It was later followed by an "Actress" robot, EveR3.

EveR-1 is made to look as close to a living, breathing human as possible. It was created as a(n) **7.** _____ to human workers. It could **8.** _____ children who are learning to read or give guided tours in museums. The designers of EveR-1 also aim to put a service robot in every home. A(n) **9.** _____ service robot can be used for many things, like cleaning the house and providing entertainment.

B. Words in Context. Complete each sentence with the best answer.

1. If something is dangerous, it isn't _____.
  a. quiet b. safe

2. If you operate a machine, you _____ it.
  a. use b. fix

3. If you aid a person, you _____ that person.
  a. hurt b. help

4. If ground is rough, it is _____ to walk on.
  a. difficult b. easy

> ## Word **Partnership**
>
> Use **operate** with:
> operate **a machine**, operate **a business**, operate **a company**.

12B Future Worlds

Before You Read

A. Matching. Read about things you might find in your future home. Use the information to label the picture (**1–5**). Which do you think will really happen?

5 Cool Things in Your Future Home

1 **Fashion Helper:** What should you wear today? Is it warm or cold outside? Which shirt matches your pants? Your computer can help you decide.

2 **Virtual Chef:** Need to bake a cake for a party? The computer gives you instructions—and a virtual (not real) chef shows you how to make it!

3 **Kitchen Robots:** Oops, you spill some juice! Don't worry—a robot helper quickly comes to clean the floor.

4 **Easy Shopping:** Your milk is getting old. The kitchen computer sends a message to the store. You don't have to do a thing!

5 **Smart Clothes:** Feel like dancing? Your shirt changes its color and pattern to match the music.

B. Predict. Look at the picture on the next page. What other things will be different in the future? Read the passage to check your ideas.

How Will We Live in 2035?

1 Welcome to your future life!

You get up in the morning and look into the mirror. Your face is firm and young-looking. In 2035, medical science is better than ever. Many people your age could live to be 150, so at 40, you're not
5 old at all. And your parents just had an anti-aging nanotechnology[1] treatment. Now, all three of you look the same age!

You say to your shirt, "Turn red." It changes from blue to red. In 2035, "smart clothes" contain particles much smaller than the cells in your body. The particles can be programmed to
10 change your clothes' color or pattern.

You walk into the kitchen. You grab the milk, but a voice says, "You shouldn't drink that!" Your fridge has read the RFID chip[2] on the milk's label, and it knows the milk is old. In 2035, every food item in the grocery store has an RFID chip.

15 It's time to go to work. In 2035, cars drive themselves. Just tell your "smart car" where to go. On the way, you can call a friend using your jacket sleeve.[3] Nano-sized "smart technology" is all around you. "Your whole body and surroundings[4] [will] become part of the same network," says scientist Ampy Buchholz.

20 So will all these predictions come true? For new technology to succeed, says futurist Andrew Zolli, "it has to be so much better that it replaces what we have already." The Internet is one example— what will be the next?

> "Your whole body and surroundings [will] become part of the same network."
>
> —Ampy Buchholz, scientist

[1] **Nanotechnology** is the science of very small things that are measured by a nanometer (one billionth of a meter).
[2] A **computer chip** is a small piece of electronic equipment.
[3] The **sleeves** of a shirt, jacket, or other item of clothing are the parts that cover your arms.
[4] Your **surroundings** refer to the look and feel of the place around you.

Reading Comprehension

A. Multiple Choice. Choose the best answer for each question.

Gist
1. The article is mainly about _____.
   a. which kinds of technology people in the future will enjoy most
   b. why medical treatments of the future will improve our lives
   c. how future technology could affect everyday life
   d. what people will eat and wear in the future

Main Idea
2. What's the main idea of the third paragraph (from line 11)?
   a. In the future, people will not drink real milk.
   b. In the future, milk will stay fresh for a longer time.
   c. In the future, you will drink many things besides milk.
   d. In the future, all food items will carry information.

Reference
3. The word *that* (line 12) refers to _____.
   a. the kitchen   c. the fridge
   b. the milk   d. the label

Inference
4. Which statement would Ampy Buchholz probably agree with?
   a. People's bodies may become less strong because of nanotechnology.
   b. Nanotechnology will become very common in the future.
   c. Nano-sized particles may be dangerous to people's health.
   d. Life will be less interesting because everyone will look the same.

Detail
5. Which prediction is NOT mentioned in the article?
   a. You'll be able to use your clothes to call a friend.
   b. Clothes will be able to change their pattern.
   c. You'll be able to use your clothes to watch a video.
   d. Cars will be able to drive by themselves.

B. Labeling. Complete each label using one or two words from the reading or footnotes.

Nano-sized robots (nanobots) are so _____ that you can't see them.

People use nanotechnology to make their _____ seem young and _____.

You can easily change the _____ or _____ of your clothes.

In 2035, _____ cars can drive themselves.

You can call a friend using the _____ of your shirt or jacket.

Vocabulary Practice

A. Completion. Complete the information using words from the box. Three words are extra.

cell	patterns
drive	program
firm	replace
label	succeed
network	treatment

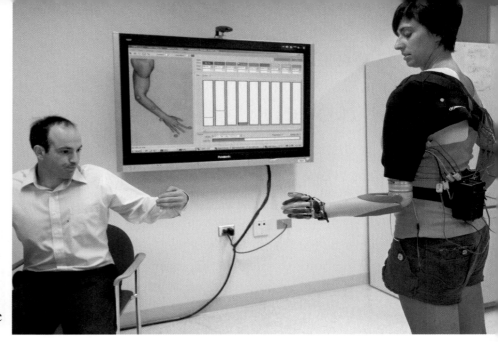

▲ Amanda Kitts learns to use the Proto 1 arm computer system, a kind of robotic arm.

Science fiction writers have long dreamed of metal bodies—people using machines to help them when their bodies fail. Now that dream is slowly becoming a reality.

Scientists discovered that even though a body part is gone, the **1.** _____ of nerves which connect it to the brain still works. With this knowledge, they can **2.** _____ machines to pick up signals from the brain, so people can operate them just by thinking about the action itself. After losing her arm in a car accident in 2006, Amanda Kitts couldn't pick up items, **3.** _____ a car, or do other everyday things. Now she has the opportunity to **4.** _____ the missing arm with a robotic one. The same principles apply to deaf or blind people. Jo Ann Lewis, a blind woman, can now see the shapes of trees using a tiny camera that connects to the nerves around her eyes.

However, this technology is still very new. Some people do not respond well to the
5. _____ and have to stop. Jo Ann Lewis, for example, still cannot see
6. _____ clearly, or even cross a road. But it won't be too long before scientists
7. _____ in joining man and machine.

B. Definitions. Use the correct form of the words in the box in **A** to complete the definitions.

1. A(n) _____ is a set of instructions for a computer to do something.

2. A(n) _____ is the smallest part of your body.

3. A(n) _____ is attached to an object and gives information about it.

4. If something is _____, it is strong and not soft.

5. A(n) _____ is a design of lines or shapes.

> ## Usage
>
> You **drive** a car, bus, or truck.
> You **ride** a bicycle or motorcycle.
> *I **ride** a bicycle to school. My brother **drives** a car to work.*

Mars Rovers

A. Preview. Read the information. Then match each word in blue with a definition.

Some people call Mars "the Red Planet." It's close to Earth, and some scientists think there might be life there. To get more information about Mars, robot explorers have landed on its surface. We have learned some surprising things from their work.

1. things that are alive _____

2. a large, round object in space that moves around the sun _____

3. the top or outside part of something _____

4. arrive somewhere after a trip _____

▲ *Spirit* and its twin robot *Opportunity* have traveled more than 20 km across the rocky surface of Mars, and have given us a lot of new information about the planet.

B. Summarize. Watch the video, *Mars Rovers*. Then complete the summary below with words from the box. Two words are extra.

aid	drive	operate	rough	single
alternative	existed	patterns	signs	whereas

C. Think About It.

1. Do you think governments should spend money for space projects like the Mars rovers? Why or why not?

2. How will technology make our lives better in the future?

The planet Mars is very interesting to scientists because it is the closest and most similar to Earth. For example, Mars has seasons with different weather, **1.** _____ other planets have the same temperatures all year round. Did life exist on Mars? To find out, scientists need to know if Mars ever had water. In 2004, two robot explorers, or "rovers," called Spirit and Opportunity were sent to Mars to look for **2.** _____ of water. These rovers can **3.** _____ over rocks and all kinds of **4.** _____ ground. They can also **5.** _____ cameras and send photos back to Earth. First, the two rovers found chemicals and **6.** _____ in the rocks that were probably made by water. Then they moved to a(n) **7.** _____ area and found other rocks which may have been created by water. Now scientists think there was probably water on the planet long ago. They still don't know if life ever **8.** _____ on Mars. But they received a lot of important information that will help them in the future.

To learn more about technology, visit elt.heinle.com/explorer

A. Crossword. Use the definitions below to complete the missing words.

Across

1. uneven, not smooth
4. only one
6. smallest part of an animal or plant
8. able or likely to hurt you
9. to help
10. to reach a goal or do well at something
13. a short distance away
15. to do something often to get better at it
17. to join together
18. medical attention given to sick or injured people
19. as good as it can possibly be

Down

2. to make a machine work, e.g., a robot
3. If you _____ to do something, you plan or hope to achieve it.
5. A _____ of something is a part of it.
6. to press something hard until it breaks
7. A _____ store is one that is in your area or town.
11. action taken to protect against attack
12. a belief about the way people should behave
14. central or most important part of something
16. The _____ of an organization are the people who work for it.

B. Notes Completion. Scan the information on pages **142–143** to complete the notes.

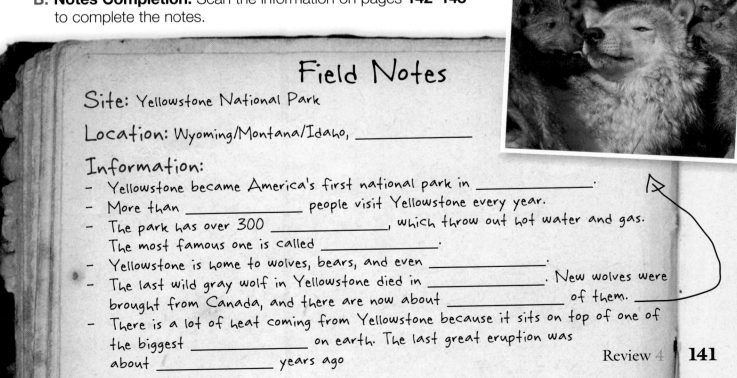

Field Notes

Site: Yellowstone National Park

Location: Wyoming/Montana/Idaho, _____

Information:
- Yellowstone became America's first national park in _____.
- More than _____ people visit Yellowstone every year.
- The park has over 300 _____, which throw out hot water and gas. The most famous one is called _____.
- Yellowstone is home to wolves, bears, and even _____.
- The last wild gray wolf in Yellowstone died in _____. New wolves were brought from Canada, and there are now about _____ of them. ____
- There is a lot of heat coming from Yellowstone because it sits on top of one of the biggest _____ on earth. The last great eruption was about _____ years ago

Smoking Wonderland

Site: **Yellowstone National Park**

Location: **Wyoming/Montana/Idaho, U.S.A.**

Category: **Natural**

Status: **World Heritage Site since 1978**

Yellowstone National Park

Yellowstone's geysers, pools, and other natural surprises have given the national park its nickname: "Wonderland."

In the early 1800s, explorers in North America came back from the west with stories about a strange land with **boiling** mud, **steaming** lakes, and trees made of stone. The stories seemed incredible—but they were true. The explorers had discovered Yellowstone. In 1872, it became America's—and the world's—first National Park.

Today, more than two million people visit Yellowstone National Park every year. One of the most popular sights is its famous **geyser** called Old Faithful, which **erupts** every 90 minutes, day and night. The park has more than 300 other geysers—more than 60% of all the geysers in the world. There are also pools of hot mud, and hot blue lakes with steam above them.

Because Yellowstone is full of warm places in the winter, it is the home of many kinds of animals and plants. Visitors to the park have the opportunity to see wolves, bears, and, if they are lucky, a mountain lion. Just be careful where you walk: every year, some visitors are burned by hot mud or water.

The last wild wolf in Yellowstone was killed in 1926. Nearly 70 years later, 14 wolves from Canada were caught and brought to live in the park. Since then, the number of wolves living in Yellowstone has risen to about 300.

Glossary

ash: gray dust produced after something is burned

boil: change from liquid to vapor (e.g., steam, smoke, or gas) by applying heat

erupt: throw out a lot of very hot material

geyser: a hole in the earth where hot water and gas come out

steam: very hot water that becomes a gas

Ready to Blow?

Where does all Yellowstone's heat come from? The national park sits on top of one of the largest—and most dangerous—volcanoes on Earth.

ALEJANDRO TUMAS, NG STAFF; SHELLEY SPERRY; NGM MAPS
SOURCES: ATLAS OF YELLOWSTONE, UNIVERSITY OF OREGON AND YELLOWSTONE
NATIONAL PARK (MAIN MAP); ROBERT L. CHRISTIANSEN AND KENNETH L. PIERCE, USGS

Yellowstone's largest eruption 640,000 years ago was a thousand times stronger than the 1980 eruption of Mt. St. Helens. Winds carried ash across much of the western United States, and the Earth's climate became darker and cooler. Scientists believe that Yellowstone's "super-volcano" will erupt again, but it could be 100,000 years in the future.

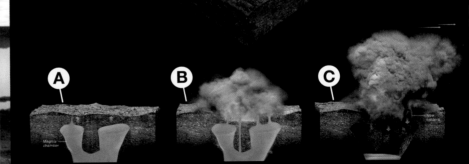

Beneath Yellowstone is an area of super-heated rock called a magma chamber (**A**). Pressure deep within the earth causes the magma to rise (**B**). When the volcano erupts, it can cause ash and other material to rise 40 kilometers (25 miles) into the air (**C**). The result, says scientist Bob Christiansen, is like "opening the Coke bottle after you've shaken it."

A. Word Partnership. Read the passage below and underline any phrases containing the word *set*. Then use the phrases to complete the sentences (**1–6**).

1. If you _____ something, you keep or save it for a purpose.

2. If you _____ on a journey, you start it.

3. If you _____ something, like an organization, you create it.

4. If you _____ for something, you are the best at it.

5. If you _____ rules for something, you decide what can and can't be done.

6. If you _____ something, you see it, usually for the first time.

On September 3, 2007, wildlife conservationist Mike Fay set out on a year-long hike through California's redwood forests. Fay **decided to** do the 1,000-kilometer (620-mile) walk for a clear purpose: he **hoped to** find a way to balance timber[1] production with redwood conservation.

Redwoods are the oldest, tallest trees on the planet, and the Redwood National Forest contains half of them. One tree called Hyperion even set the record for the tallest known living thing at 115 meters (375 feet). The first European to set eyes on the forests was Fray Juan Crespi in 1769. Just 80 years later, people started cutting down trees as the need for timber rose. Over the next hundred years, most of the 800,000 hectares (two million acres) of old redwood forest were cut down.

In 1904, President Theodore Roosevelt **agreed to** set aside redwood land in California as a public park. However, people still cut down the trees. The Save-the-Redwoods league was set up in response. They **offered to** buy over land for conservation, with the help of National Geographic Society and Sierra Club. In 1968, the U.S. government finally set down laws to create what is now the Redwood National Park. They **plan to** enlarge the park further to protect more trees.

[1] **Timber** is wood used for building houses, tables, chairs, etc.

B. Word Partnership. Read the passage again and note the five **verb + to** combinations in red. Use the combinations to complete the sentences below. Some sentences can use more than one combination.

1. When Robert Ballard returned to *Titanic*, he _____ find the wreck in good condition, but he was disappointed.

2. NASA _____ use robot snakes as an alternative to vehicles with wheels.

3. A group called OLPC has _____ give free laptops to children in poor countries.

4. Sacagawea _____ help Lewis and Clark by joining their expedition.

5. Christopher Duffy _____ climb Mt. Bukhansan even though it was crowded.

6. While on Mt. Bukhansan, Duffy met some people who _____ share their food with him.

▲ This 90-meter (300-foot) redwood in California is over 1,500 years old.

Target Vocabulary

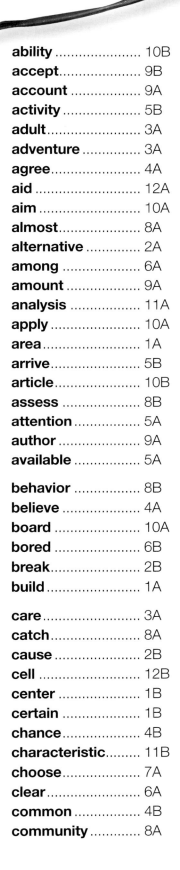

Target Vocabulary

Target Vocabulary

1 Loch Ness Mystery

Narrator:

Loch Ness, a lake in Scotland, is an area of great natural beauty. But it is perhaps best known as the home of a monster, called Nessie . . .

Nessie has a long history going back more than a thousand years, when people first reported a strange movement in the lake. But it wasn't until a number of sightings in the 1930s that Nessie really became famous. Newspapers in London published stories about the monster. But there was a problem—they didn't have any pictures.

In 1934, this image—from a London doctor named R. Kenneth Wilson— was published in several newspapers and books. It made many people certain that Nessie was real—and the Loch Ness story continued to grow.

Then, nearly 60 years later, a man named Christian Spurling finally told the true story. He said the photo was the work of his stepfather, "Duke" Wetherall.

A newspaper in London had sent Wetherall to Loch Ness to take a photo of the monster.

When Wetherall didn't see anything, he lost his job. So Wetherall decided to design and build his own monster. He made a monster's head and placed it on a simple toy submarine. He put it in the water, and took a photo. Then he got Dr. Wilson to say that he had taken the picture.

Although the photo wasn't real, that hasn't stopped thousands of people from coming to Loch Ness, hoping to see for themselves if there really is a monster in the lake.

A Taste of Mexico

Narrator:
Visitors to the historic city of Oaxaca can experience amazing colors and sounds, and wonderful smells. It's a place that's famous for its beauty and traditions. Although it's one of the poorest states in Mexico, Oaxaca is rich in culture. And what makes Oaxaca really special is its food.

Susana Trilling:
"It's one of the best foods. It's very complex."

Narrator:
Susana Trilling loved the chilies in Oaxacan food. So she moved to Oaxaca to start her own cooking school. Susana's students heard about Oaxacan food in their own countries and joined her to learn how to produce and serve real Oaxacan dishes.

Oaxacan food developed a long time before people came from Europe to America. For Trilling, it's this long tradition that helps keep the food alive. She says that Oaxacan food—with its many different ingredients—can be as complex as Thai food or French food.

An important step in cooking Oaxacan food is making a sauce called mole. Made from chili peppers, chocolate, and other ingredients, mole is standard in various Oaxacan dishes.

But Oaxacan culture is more than just food. The state is also famous for its dances. This dance is centuries old. It's called the Guelagetza. It tells about the culture, history, and music of the Oaxacan people.

Many of the buildings in the city are Mexican national treasures. This building, with its archways, gardens, and fountains, is 500 years old. In the past, it was a government building. Today, it's a top-price hotel.

Oaxacan people say that a healthy person is someone who is happy, at peace, and who loves to work and eat. After experiencing just a short stay in Oaxaca, you can see that the tradition is still very much alive.

3 History of Film

Narrator:

For more than a hundred years, film has entertained people around the world. Movies let us see new things, experience history, and dream about living like the actors on a movie screen.

In the 19th century, inventors learned that they could create moving images by showing a series of pictures very quickly. In 1891, in the United States, Thomas Edison and William Dickson designed and created a machine called a kinetoscope. People could pay a fee to look into the machine and watch simple movies. Before long, a machine called a projector could show movies to large groups of people.

People loved this new technology. Everyday life was much more exciting when it was shown in a movie. The first movies were of simple things like trains, but these were soon followed by movies with longer and more complex stories. By the 1920s, several movie studios had opened in Hollywood, California. Crowds of people went to see their productions, and new "movie palaces" were built to show them in. Actors like Mary Pickford and Charlie Chaplin became famous around the world.

But outside of Hollywood, film was being used in other ways, allowing us to experience the world in a different way. At the beginning of the 20th century, movie directors began to record real happenings and important events. They filmed presidents, explorers, and any kind of human experience, including the Wright Brothers' early flights.

In the hands of filmmakers, cameras can also show us the traditions of people living in other parts of the planet, and take us far away from our homes. Since those early days, documentary filmmakers have learned to use film in ways that explain how the world really is.

Technology can help us see things much faster than they really happen. It can also let us see things much more slowly, like the movement of a hawk. In the future, film technology may show us new ways to understand the world.

Over the years, ideas from Hollywood have helped documentary filmmakers develop their art. Actors, lighting, and even computer animation are now used to teach us about the real world. Now we can experience other places and other times in history in ways people before us could only dream of.

In only a hundred years, film making has changed completely. Those early simple pictures have now become our window to the world.

Lightning

4

Narrator:

Lightning is a common natural event—one that scientists are still learning about.

You're most likely to see lightning in summer, when it breaks the peace and quiet of a hot day.

Around the world, lightning happens 50 to 100 times a second. Lightning happens most often in Central Africa, the Himalayas, and South America.

We can often see lightning flashing between storm clouds and the earth.

Lightning is electricity. Scientists don't fully agree about why the lightning escapes from the cloud. But they generally agree that lightning occurs because of electricity moving up and down inside the cloud. Some particles move to the top of the cloud and get a positive charge. Other particles move down and get a negative charge. The positive and negative charges get stronger, and this creates electricity—lightning—between the two parts of the cloud.

Lightning mainly stays inside the cloud, but sometimes it reaches the earth. The energy of the lightning is very strong, but it is finished after less than a second. Lightning looks like one flash coming down, but it's really a series of return flashes reaching back into the cloud.

Inside the lightning, the temperature is more than 28,000 degrees Celsius. This high temperature changes the pressure inside the lightning, and that makes the sound of thunder.

In the United States, you're most likely to see lighting in Florida. The hot, wet weather conditions there create thunder clouds, and these clouds produce lightning.

Lightning is nature at its most dangerous. Every year, it causes about 100 deaths in the United States—more than hurricanes or tornadoes. If you're in a lightning storm, you should go inside a building, or get in a car, and wait for the storm to end. As a rule, it's best to stay away from high places and tall trees.

Lightning is a natural and common event, but one that can be deadly.

5 Dubai World Cup

Narrator:
Several of the world's best racehorses are arriving on the track to practice, and it's still only five o'clock in the morning.

Nick Robb:
"I started at four o'clock this morning, and we usually finish about nine o'clock. The reason we do it at that time of the morning is basically because it's cooler for the horses. It's quieter."

Narrator:
The air usually gets very hot in the Arabian Gulf, with temperatures reaching 40 degrees Celsius.

Nick Robb:
"They get used to it, like I do, getting up in the middle of the night."

Narrator:
Nick Robb runs the Oasis Stables, owned by the royal family of Dubai, the Maktoums.

Nick says the easiest way to describe training a race horse is that it's almost the same as training to run a race, or getting ready for an Olympic Games.

Horses are athletes. But these are special athletes, and they get a lot of attention. For example, a horse named "Conflict" goes out to a small track to run—and then he enjoys a wash. Special ice boots are available to keep his legs in good condition.

In the afternoon, the crowd starts to fill the modern stadium in Dubai. Today there will be seven different races—including the Dubai World Cup. Its prize of six million dollars is the biggest in the world. The Dubai World Cup isn't very old, but horse racing traditions go back for hundreds of years in Arabia.

Les Benton:
"Well, there is a culture of love of horses, as seen through the Arabian horse, and the Arab people in general have a love of horses and they have a love of competition and they like to see the horses race."

Narrator:
A few hundred years ago, Arabian horses were introduced in Europe to create a new kind of racehorse. These horses are called thoroughbreds and they are some of the fastest racehorses in the world. Today, the royal family of Dubai has many of the world's top thoroughbreds.

Simon Crisford runs the Godolphin stables for the royal family's racehorses. He says they have the best stables, the best trainers, and, he hopes, the best team in the world. A couple of his horses have a good chance at being race leaders today.

Simon Crisford:
"With the Dubai World Cup being the richest horse race in the whole world, and we've got a great chance of winning it, so we're very excited."

Narrator:
Many people at the stadium are from Dubai while others are foreign. Some wear traditional clothes—and others more modern—including some unusual hats.

After one race, the winners are introduced to Sheik Mohammed Maktoum from the royal family. And finally, at the end of the night, a horse named "Street Cry" wins the big prize—the Dubai World Cup.

Native Americans

Narrator:

They were the first people in North America. We don't know when they arrived, or the reason for their movement. But many scientists believe that 30,000 years ago, people from Asia walked or sailed along land that used to join Russia and North America.

We don't have full knowledge of their history, but these people were the first Native Americans, or American Indians.

The Native Americans moved across the land and changed their way of living in places with different conditions. They became hundreds of different groups, with different languages and ways of living. In some places, the Indians lived by hunting buffalo. Near the Pacific Ocean, they caught fish instead, and sailed in boats. They used the tall trees to build villages, boats, and traditional art called totem poles.

When the first white people arrived in the 1500s, there was a healthy population of about one million Native Americans living north of Mexico. But things were different once the foreigners arrived. They brought European diseases which caused many deaths among the Indians.

The settlers wanted to take the Indians' land. Some groups accepted the white people, and others tried to fight. But in the end, they lost their land. In the late 1800s, the United States government told the Indians to leave their homes and live on sites called reservations.

Over the next hundred years, Native Americans continued to fight for a better life.

Today, there are more than 550 recognized tribes or nations in the United States. Some have held meetings with the government to discuss returning their land.

Native Americans are working towards better living conditions on the reservations. They also want to keep their languages, religions, and cultural identities. This ceremony is called a "potlatch."

In the past, the ceremony was stopped by the Canadian government. Now the Kwakiutl nation is performing it again.

The Navajo nation also mixes old and modern ways. This painting represents the cloud people. The artist is making it to keep a group of people safe while they travel on a plane.

Many Native American artists are bringing back traditional art forms—and helping their culture to grow stronger in the future.

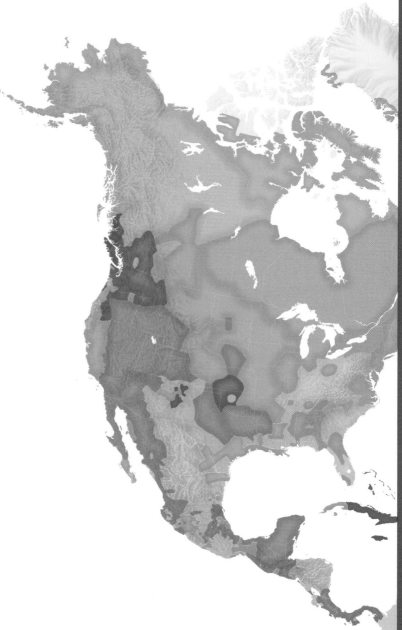

7 Parasomnia

Narrator:

For most people, sleeping is easy and straightforward. For others, it can be a real nightmare!

Some people dream of being attacked and may even fight with their partners while they sleep. Other people get up and walk around in their sleep—without knowing what they are doing. These sleep conditions—called parasomnia—can be dangerous.

Scientists are hoping to find out why they occur.

Parasomnia happens during the period before REM sleep. REM sleep is the stage of sleep when we dream. The time before this is when people may sleep-walk, sleep-talk, or even sleep-eat. Yet they have no knowledge of their activities.

Parasomnia happens during a time in the sleep cycle called NREM or non-REM: Non-Rapid Eye Movement. NREM contains four stages. During stage one, your brain is producing small waves, and you are in a light sleep. In stage two, your body relaxes and your heartbeat and breathing gets slower. The brain waves are larger and become further apart. The deepest sleep is during stages three and four. For most of us, our brains shut off sounds and movement from the outside world.

But for sleepwalkers, the lower part of the brain "wakes up," while the upper part—the thinking brain, or the mind—is asleep. This is why sleepwalkers are able to move around at night, and yet they don't remember it the next day. With further research, scientists hope one day to fully explain this mysterious event.

Penguins in Trouble

Narrator:

In Antarctica, every day is a fight for survival.

This community of emperor penguins has been fishing for two weeks. This is necessary as the parents have to bring back a lot of food to raise their hungry babies. But—they are in danger.

A leopard seal waits nearby. It's hungry, too. Some penguins jump safely onto land before it can catch them. The leopard seal waits . . . and assesses the situation.

More penguins arrive. But they have sensed the dangerous leopard seal, so they turn around fast.

Now more and more penguins take their chance and jump onto the ice. The penguins are getting away— until the leopard seal decides to join them. The penguins try to get away.

Out of their usual environment in the water, the seal and penguins have a similar problem. They cannot move very fast.

The leopard seal catches a penguin and it seems obvious that it has won. But the penguins have a special escape plan. They don't fight—if they are caught, they simply relax their bodies. The seal accidently drops this lucky penguin, and it quickly gets away. It returns safely to its friends.

But the leopard seal doesn't give up so easily and keeps trying. It catches another penguin. This time, it's successful, and the leopard seal enters the sea with its prize.

9 Lost Treasure of Afghanistan

Narrator:

Afghanistan—a country rich in history, and in beautiful ancient art.

But in the last 30 years, a series of wars has led to many of Afghanistan's treasures being lost or broken up. One important treasure which was almost lost is the valuable Bactrian Hoard.

In 1978, a Russian archeologist named Victor Sarianidi went to Afghanistan to dig for ancient pots. Instead, he found the tombs of a royal family, filled with large amounts of gold of the highest quality.

Viktor Sarianidi:

"When we found the second and then the third tomb, I started asking myself how come it was me, a little boy from Tashkent, who discovered the gold of the world? Could I be that lucky?"

Narrator:

Victor recorded over 20,000 gold items which were 2,000 years old. Newspaper reports described it as one of the greatest discoveries ever made.

But war was coming to Afghanistan. The archeologists quickly took the gold treasures out of the ground, and moved them to the National Museum in Kabul. Soon after, fighting began in Kabul, and the National Museum was bombed. The Bactrian Hoard disappeared. No one knew where it went to.

Over the years, people started talking. Some said the army demanded the gold for financial reasons. Others said that Victor Sarianidi took it—a story that made him sad and angry.

In 2003, the war was over, and Afghanistan began to return to normal. The new leader of Afghanistan, Hamid Karzai, heard about a secret room in the presidential palace with many boxes. Did the room contain the Bactrian gold?

National Geographic archeologist Fred Hiebert had the opportunity to visit Kabul to look inside the secret room. His teacher, Victor Sarianidi, accepted Fred's offer to go with him. But when they went to the palace, they received some bad news.

Fred Hiebert:

"And we said, 'Well, what are we waiting for?' They said, 'There's no keys to the boxes.' We said, 'There are no keys to the boxes?' They said, 'Yes, the keys are with the key-holders, and the key-holders are gone.' The key-holders—they're called talwidars—are the keepers of the treasures of Afghanistan. And in this particular case, the key-holders were gone, and without the key-holders nobody in the country had the right to open the boxes."

Narrator:

These key-holders were supposed to be the only people who could open the boxes. But, since they were gone, President Karzai gave instructions to open the boxes.

The archeologists were worried about the treasure.

Fred Hiebert:

"My heart was just trembling. I was worried about the gold. I was worried about the artifacts. I was worried about everything."

Narrator:

Finally, one of boxes was opened—and the first thing they saw was a gold hairpin. It was indeed part of the Bactrian gold—lost for so many years, it was now back again.

Viktor Sarianidi:

"It's like seeing an old friend again after 25 years. You didn't even know if he is still alive. And now you realize he is right here waiting for you."

Narrator:

Today, thanks to Viktor Sarianidi and Fred Hiebert, and the people who protected the boxes, the world has the opportunity to enjoy these beautiful treasures of art and history.

Maasai Teacher

Narrator:
This is Joseph Lekuton. He's a teacher in Northern Virginia. He gives lectures to his students about the history of their country—but his country is very different.

Lekuton is a Maasai tribesman. He was born in a small village in northern Kenya. Like all Maasai boys, he took care of his family's cattle. Even now, as an adult, he still goes back to Kenya every summer, to work with the cattle.

He says that his early life was very different from American children. By the time he was seven, he was out of the house and had to learn skills like how to survive in the wild. By the time he was ten, his job was to take care of the cattle all day.

But Lekuton was also different from other Maasai children. He went to school and he practiced his English. Later, he went to college in the United States and got a job as a teacher.

Now he has written about his life in two countries in a book called "Facing the Lion." The book's title refers to an event in his childhood, when he came face to face with a lion.

Joseph Lekuton:
"The symbol of bravery in my community is the lion. Having faced that lion when I was 14 sort of changed everything for me. So . . . I think we all face challenges in life and we all have our own lions."

Narrator:
Lekuton shares stories from his Maasai childhood to help kids learn about a culture that's very different from their own, and also principles that they can apply in their own lives.

This project is Lekuton's first book. His aim is to connect traditional Maasai life and modern American life, and to show children the importance of strength and hope even if their lives are difficult.

Joseph Lekuton:
"The information I would like them to get from my book is hope. It's determination. It's courage. It's facing your lions. And all I'm trying to tell them is, I conquered, I tried to conquer some of my lions. So can you."

11 Dinosaurs

Narrator:

These scientists are digging for fossils. Fossilized bones tell the story of dinosaurs—animals that once lived on earth, beginning about 225 million years ago. Dinosaurs lived on the planet for 150 million years—much longer than humans have been around.

Imagine if the sequence of time from the moment dinosaurs appeared until now could be shown in a single day. At midnight, dinosaurs first walk the earth. They're at their prime at noon . . . and die out around five in the afternoon. The first modern humans only appear a minute and a half before midnight.

Dinosaurs had many different shapes and sizes. The smallest dinosaur was less than one meter long. The largest were giants called sauropods. This sauropod called *jobaria* was longer than a city bus and weighed more than 22 thousand kilograms, about 50 thousand pounds. It had to eat a lot of plants every day. The plants passed through a throat six meters long—the animal's neck was as tall as a house! Each step jobaria took was heavy enough to crush a car.

Although many dinosaurs were huge, they share some characteristics with modern animals. For example, most dinosaurs laid eggs. This dinosaur died while she was sitting on her eggs. Her partner probably brought food to her, like birds do. The mother also moved the eggs into a circle, much like a bird.

Some dinosaurs ate plants. As they had no way to defend themselves against meat-eating dinosaurs, they lived together in groups.

But 65 million years ago, something happened which caused the dinosaurs to go extinct.

No one knows exactly why, but all the dinosaurs suddenly disappeared. Most scientists think a giant rock from space may have hit the earth. This sent a lot of dust into the air and reduced the amount of sunlight. The planet became cold and dark, causing the dinosaurs to die off.

Dinosaurs may not be around anymore, but scientists believe they may live on . . . in birds. The bones of some dinosaurs, like these, are very similar to the bones of modern birds.

They are probably related to small, two-legged, meat-eating dinosaurs.

Ongoing research and fossil analysis is trying to determine the connection between birds and dinosaurs. Maybe dinosaurs aren't really extinct. Maybe birds are really living, breathing, and flying dinosaurs.

Mars Rovers

Narrator:

Labeled the "Red Planet" for its fiery color, Mars has so far been too far away—and dangerous—for humans to explore. The alternative has been to build robots to aid scientists in their research. In 2004, two robot explorers, or rovers, called Spirit and Opportunity, were sent to Mars. Their mission was to find signs of water.

Spirit landed first, after a seven-month trip. It was to explore an area scientists believed was once a lake. Opportunity landed three weeks later in another place with different rocks. These rovers can drive over rough ground and operate cameras and scientific instruments. They set out to work.

Mars is important to scientists because it is close to Earth and similar in many ways. Mars has seasons with different kinds of weather. It also has a network of what looks like dried rivers and lakes. This has raised the question—was there once life on Mars?

Most scientists hold a firm belief that all life needs water. To look for water, the robots carried equipment to measure the chemicals in rocks. As well as being equipped with solar power cells, the rovers also carried special cameras for scientists to record images of the planet's rocks.

After only two months, scientists had found what they were looking for. Opportunity found chemicals and patterns in the rocks that showed the area was full of water a long time ago. Scientists don't know when this happened or how much water there was, but the surprising discovery changed their ideas about Mars. Now they believe that the weather on Mars was once warmer, maybe warm enough to once have forms of life.

In the following months, Spirit moved on to an area that may once have been a volcano, whereas Opportunity went on to study rocks that may have formed underwater.

Today, scientists still aren't sure if life ever existed on Mars. They need more information to decide. The discoveries of the two Mars rovers answered some old questions—but they also brought up many new ones.

Photo Credits

1 Michael Nichols/NGIC, 3 Jim Richardson/NGIC, 4, 5 (clockwise from t-l) Michael Melford/NGIC, Raymond Wong/Skaramoosh Ltd., Tyson Mangelsdorf/NGIC, International Mammoth Committee, Mitsuaki Iwago/Minden Pictures/NGIC, Justin Guariglia/NGIC, David Grove/NGIC, 6, 7 (clockwise from t-l) Cary Wolinsky/NGIC, Bill Ellzey/NGIC, Michael S. Lewis/NGIC, Shakko/Wikimedia Commons, Michael Wesch, Ralph Lee Hopkins/NGIC, Mark Thiessen/NGIC, Emory Kristof/NGIC, Kyodo/Landov, Joel Sartore/NGIC, Mitsuaki Iwago/Minden Pictures/NGIC, Fred Bavendam/Minden Pictures/NGIC, Honda Motor Europe Ltd., International Mammoth Committee, Bruce Dale/NGIC, 8 (t) Michael Melford/NGIC, (b) Steve Winter/NGIC, 9 Alaska Stock Images/NGIC, 10 Columbia/The Kobal Collection, 11 (t) Bouzou/Shutterstock, (c) Peter Essick/NGIC, (b) x51/Flickr, 12 Bouzou/Shutterstock, 13 Panoramic Images/NGIC, 14 (b-l) travellinglight/iStockphoto, (b-r) Marie-Lan Nguyen/Wikimedia Commons, 17 (t) B. Anthony Stewart/NGIC, (b) Meg Forbes/Shutterstock, 18 Keystone/Stringer/Hulton Archive/Getty Images, 19 Bill Ellzey/NGIC 20 Elena Schweitzer/Shutterstock 21 (t) Afina_ok/Shutterstock, (b) Jeff Kubina/Flickr, 23 Justin Guariglia/NGIC, 24 (from l) ILCPhoto/iStockphoto, Jamesmcq24/iStockphoto, HQPhotos/iStockphoto, Quayside/iStockphoto, Mark Thiessen/NGIC, 25 (t) Frank Chang/Shutterstock (b) Strdel/AFP/Getty Images, 26 (from l) ILCPhoto/iStockphoto, HQPhotos/iStockphoto, Jamesmcq24/iStockphoto, 27 (t) Robert Clark/NGIC, (b) Robert B. Goodman/NGIC, 28 Kent Kobersteen/NGIC, 29 Michael Nichols/NGIC, 30–32 (all) Joel Sartore/NGIC, 33 Steve Winter/NGIC, 35, 36 Eriko Sugita/Reuters/Landov, 37 Jin Liangkuai/Xinhua/Landov, 38 Justin Locke/NGIC, 39–41 (all photos) Robert Clark/NGIC 42 Justin Locke/NGIC, 43 Bruce Dale/NGIC, 45 (t-inset) Emory Kristof/NGIC, (b) O. Louis Mazzatenta/NGIC, 47 Topical Press Agency/Stringer/Hulton Archive/Getty Images, 49 (t), 50 Rex A. Stucky/NGIC, (b) Justin Sagarsee/Mile High Newspapers, 51 (t-l) Brian J. Skerry/NGIC, (t-r) David Doubilet/NGIC, (b-l) Fred Bavendam/Minden Pictures/NGIC, 52 Mike Theiss/NGIC, 53 Mark Coslett/NGIC 54 Peter Kim/Shutterstock, 55 (b/g) sadrak/iStockphoto, (l) Kyodo/Landov, (r) Steve King/CSM/Landov 57 Rebecca Hale/NGIC 58, 60 (all) Korea Tourism Organization, 59 (all) Bill Dickens, 61 Darlyne A. Murawski/NGIC, 62 Melissa Farlow/NGIC, 63 Chris Johns/NGIC, 64 (clockwise from t-l) Ira Block/NGIC (first 2), Ralph E. Gray/NGIC, mattesimages/Shutterstock, 66 hidesy/iStockphoto, 67 (b) Kenneth Garrett/NGIC, 68 (t) Paul Sutherland/NGIC, (b-from l) Jason Edwards/NGIC (first 2), Cyril Ruoso/JH Editorial/Minden Pictures/NGIC, (and 70) Fred Bavendam/Minden Pictures/NGIC, Robert Clark/NGIC, 69 (t) Annie Griffiths Belt/NGIC, (b) zbindere/iStockphoto, 71 Shakko/Wikimedia Commons, 73 Gerry Ellis/Minden Pictures/NGIC, 74–75 (b/g) Mitsuaki Iwago/Minden Pictures/NGIC, 75 (t) Annie Griffiths Belt/NGIC, (b) Gerry Ellis/Minden Pictures/NGIC, 76 Yves Rossy/http://www.jet-man.com, 77 Nick Norman/NGIC, 78 Richard Nowitz/NGIC, 81 Joel Sartore/NGIC, 82 Yakobchuk Vasyl/Shutterstock, 83 Charles Knox/Shutterstock, 85 James L. Stanfield/NGIC, 86 Alex James Bramwell/Shutterstock, 87, 88, 90 Konrad Wothe/Minden Pictures/NGIC, 89 (t) Tui De Roy/Minden Pictures/NGIC, (c, b) Konrad Wothe/Minden Pictures/NGIC, 91 Marc Moritsch/NGIC, 92 (clockwise from t-l) Kenneth Love/NGIC, Joel Sartore/NGIC, Gerry Ellis/Minden Pictures/NGIC, Tom Murphy/NGIC, Karine Aigner/NGIC, Alaska Stock Images/NGIC, 93 (l) Vincent J. Musi/NGIC, (r) Yva Momatiuk & John Eastcott/Minden Pictures/NGIC, 95 Vincent J. Musi/NGIC, 96 Flip De Nooyer/Foto Natura/Minden Pictures/NGIC, 97 James P. Blair/NGIC, 98 (c) Stephen Alvarez/NGIC, (b) Stuart Franklin/NGIC, 100 Stephen Alvarez/NGIC, 101 Jeanyfan/Wikimedia Commons, 102 (b), 104 Cary Wolinsky/NGIC, 103 (t) B. Anthony Stewart/NGIC, (b) Isidore Stanislas Helman/Wikimedia Commons, 105 BESTWEB/Shutterstock, 106 Kenneth Garrett/NGIC, 107, 108 Justin Guariglia/NGIC, 108–9 (b/g) Michael S. Lewis/NGIC, 109 Wikimedia Commons, 110 Tim Fitzharris/Minden Pictures/NGIC, 111 Steve McCurry/NGIC, 112 (t-l) Chris Johns/NGIC, (b-l, r) Paul Sutherland/NGIC,

113 (all) Anthony de Boer/Southern Cross Wildlife School, 115 Raul Touzon/NGIC, 116 Justin Guariglia/NGIC, 117 (t) Alaska Stock Images/NGIC, (b) Michael Wesch, 119 One Laptop Per Child/Flickr, 120 Randy Olsen/NGIC, 122, 123 (t) International Mammoth Committee, 125 George Steinmetz/NGIC, 129 Tsunemi Kubodera/AP, 130 (all) Roy Anderson/NGIC, 131 Jim Richardson/NGIC, 132 George Steinmetz/NGIC, 133 (t-all) Honda Motor Europe Ltd., (b) Robert Clark/NGIC, 135 You Sung-Ho/Reuters/Landov, 139 Max Aguilera-Hellweg/NGIC, 140 NASA, 141, 142 Norbert Rosing/NGIC, 142–3 (b/g) Michael Melford/NGIC, 144 Michael Nichols/NGIC, 145 Frans Lanting/NGIC, 148 Keystone/Stringer/Hulton Archive/Getty Images, 149 Kent Kobersteen/NGIC, 150 Justin Locke/NGIC, 151 Mike Theiss/NGIC, 152 Melissa Farlow/NGIC, 154 Alex James Bramwell/Shutterstock, 155 Flip De Nooyer/Foto Natura/Minden Pictures/NGIC, 156 Kenneth Garrett/NGIC, 157 Randy Olsen/NGIC, 158 Roy Anderson/NGIC, 159 NASA

Illustration Credits

11, 17, 18, 21, 25, 28, 31, 34, 40, 48, 49, 59, 61, 62, 64, 69, 72, 74, 89, 96, 98, 99, 102, 106, 108, 113, 115, 120, 122, 142, 143, 153 National Geographic Maps, 14 (t), 16 Jörg Röse-oberreich/Shutterstock, 15 Tyson Mangelsdorf, 41 (t) Jerome N. Cockson & Lisa R. Ritter/NG Staff, (b) Fernando G. Baptista/NG Staff, 44, 45 (t), 46 Raymond Wong/Skaramoosh/NG Staff, 65 (all) David Grove/NGIC, 67 (t) Fernando G. Baptista/NGIC, 83 (b) Blake Thornton, 98 (t) H. M. Herget/NGIC, 99 Ned M. Seidler/NGIC, 121 Raul Martin/NGIC, 122–124 Kazuhiko Sano/NGIC, 126–8 (all) Matte FX/NGIC, 133 (c), 136–8 (all) Mondolithic Studios, 143 Alejandro Tumas/NG Staff & Shelley Sperry

Text Credits

11 Adapted from "UFO Mystery," by Elisabeth Deffner: NGK, Mar 2008, 15 Adapted from "Unsolved Mystery: Atlantis," by Michael N. Smith and Debora L. Smith: NGK, Mar 2005, 21 Adapted from "A Slice of History," by Susan E. Goodman: NGE, May 2005, 25 Adapted from "Hot Pod," by Catherine L. Barker: NGM, May 2007, 31 Adapted from "Grin and Bear It," by Russell Chadwick: NG World, Feb 2001, 35 Adapted from "Anime-nia!," by Jamie Kiffel: NGK, Jan/Feb 2003, 45 Adapted from "Why is Titanic Vanishing?," by Robert D. Ballard: NGM, Dec 2004, 49 Adapted from "'I Was Struck by Lightning!'," by Laura Daily: NGK, Aug 2005, 55 Adapted from "Worldwide, It's a Hit," by John L. Eliot: NGM, Apr 2004, 59 Adapted from "If You Go Hiking in Korea, Don't Forget the Vodka," by Christopher Duffy: Glimpse, 17 Mar 2009, 65 Adapted from "Who was Sacagawea?," by Dana Jensen: NGE, Mar 2007, and "Searching for Sacagawea," by Margaret Talbot: NGM, Feb 2003, 79 Adapted from "Optical Illusions": NGE, Apr 2005, 83 Adapted from "How to Decode Your Dreams," by Sarah Wassner: NGK, Aug 2005, 89 Adapted from "Destination Antarctica: Emperor Penguins," by Crispin Boyer: NGK, Apr 2009, 93 Adapted from "What's So Funny?," by Aline Alexander Newman: NGK, Apr 2006, 99 Adapted from "Lost Inca Gold: Ransom, Riches, and Riddles," by James Owen: NG Website (www.nationalgeographic.com/history/ancient/lost-inca-gold.html), 103 Adapted from "Curse of the Hope Diamond," by Kristin Baird Rattini: NGK, Oct 2006, and "Diamonds: The Real Story," by Andrew Cockburn: NGM, Mar 2002, 113 Adapted from "Game-Filled Park Is School for South African Kids," by Leon Marshall: NG News (http://news.nationalgeographic.com/news), Jan 31, 2005, 123 Adapted from "Mystery of the Frozen Mammoth," by Kristin Baird Rattini: NGK, May 2009, and "Ice Baby," by Tom Mueller: NGM, May 2009, 127 Adapted from "Sea Monster": NGE, Mar 2006, and "When Monsters Ruled the Deep," by Virginia Morell: NGM, Dec 2005, 133 Adapted from "Robot Revolution," by Douglas E. Richards: NGK, Feb 2008, and "Robot World," by Sean Price: NGK, Jan/Feb 2003, 137 Adapted from "It's 2035," by Ruth Musgrave: NGK, Sep 2005

National Geographic = NG;
National Geographic Image Collection = NGIC;
National Geographic Kids = NGK;
National Geographic Magazine = NGM;
National Geographic Explorer = NGE